Bismillah

Teaching and Learning from an Islamic Perspective

Jameela Ho, Aishah Ho, Meenara Khan, Mariam Seddiq, and Taherah Moslih

Djarabi Kitabs Publishing
Dallas, Texas
USA

Copyright

TEACHING AND LEARNING FROM AN ISLAMIC PERSPECTIVE

© 2022 Jameela Ho, Aishah Ho, Meenara Khan, Mariam Seddiq, Taherah Moslih. All rights reserved.

No part of this book may be reproduced in any written, electronic, recording, or photocopying without written permission of the publisher or author. The exception would be in the case of brief quotations embodied in the critical articles or reviews and pages where permission is specifically granted by the publisher or author. Although every precaution has been taken to verify the accuracy of the information contained herein, the author and publisher assume no responsibility for any errors or omissions. No liability is assumed for damages that may result from the use of information contained within.

For information contact:

DJARABI KITABS PUBLISHING

PO BOX 703733

DALLAS, TX 75370

www.djarabikitabs.com

Cover Design Concept by Authors

Full Cover by Sam Rog

ISBN-13: 978-1-947148-62-8

Category & Genre: Education/Islamic Homeschooling Books

Library of Congress Control Number: 2023932688

First Print Edition: March 2023

10 9 8 7 6 5 4 3 2 1

DEDICATION

This book is dedicated to Muslim parents and teachers and their children whom they try to educate to the best of their abilities.

CONTENTS

DEDICATION iii

CHAPTER 1 3

CHAPTER 2 11

CHAPTER 3 20

CHAPTER 4 46

CHAPTER 5 63

CHAPTER 6 77

ABOUT THE AUTHORS xci

CHAPTER 1
Memory for Learning & Quran Memorisation

Jameela Ho

The Memory Process

This model of learning is based on how the memory works (Hudmon, 2006). In this model, there are three types of memory: sensory memory, short term memory, and long term memory (see Figure 1).

Every second of our life we are bombarded with sensory information – through our senses of sight, hearing, smell, touch and taste. This is too much information for our brains to process so much of it is ignored and gets lost. What we pay attention to, gets into our short term or working memory.

Paying attention to a stimuli will get it processed into the working memory for about 20 seconds. The working memory is also called the short term memory for this reason as it doesn't last for long and only can store between 5 and 9 items of information. Paying attention to something doesn't necessarily mean that we will remember it. Unless something is done with the information it will disappear in 20 seconds.

To move information from working memory to long term memory, it needs to be actively processed. One way is to encode it by meaningfully linking it with something already existing in long term memory.

Another is to actively use the information; to think about it, consolidate, extend, modify or connect it.

Finally, the information needs to be recalled or retrieved once it's in long term memory otherwise it will be forgotten.

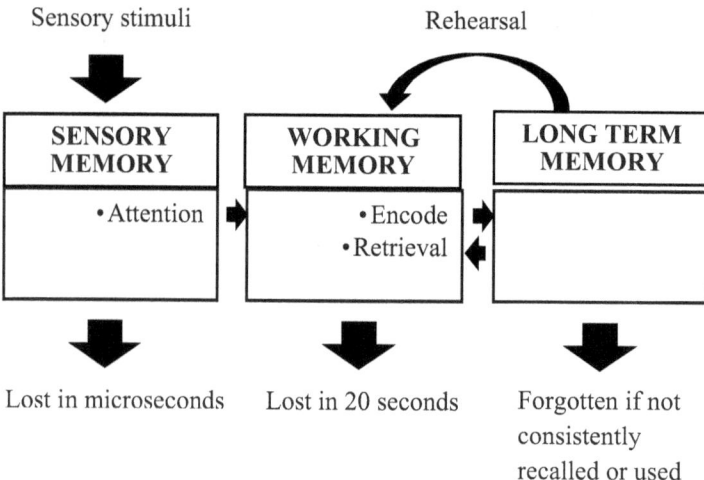

Figure 1. The Memory Process

Long Term Retention of Information

Research into how students learn found that there are three ways children should be studying for long term retention. These are retrieve what was learnt, spacing the studying and interleaving the subjects.

1. Retrieve What Was Learnt
When studying, children tend to just read over their notes or textbooks. This does not work because reading will only stay in the short term memory for a few seconds and then will disappear. What children need to do is to get it into long term memory by memorising and recalling what was read or written.

There are a few ways to help with memorising and recalling. The first is to memorise the main or important points. This will help to trigger the memory of what each point is about. Flashcards can be used to help with recall. Write the questions on one side of the cards and the answer on the other. Shuffle them and pick one card. Read the question and have your children try to answer it without looking at the answer on the back. Once they've attempted the answer by retrieving the information then they can check the answer on the back. Read *"Use Flashcards to Improve Learning"* at **http://www.ilmaeducation.com/2017/10/use-flashcards-to-improve-learning.html.**

Memory strategies such as mnemonics and pegs can also be used to help with memorisation. Read *"3 Ways to Improve Your Child's Memory to Help with Learning"* at **http://www.ilmaeducation.com/2014/09/3-ways-to-improve-your-childrens-memory.html** where I go into details of mnemonics and two others.

2. Space the Studying
Space the study periods. Don't just study one subject for long periods before the test. Don't cram. This might work in the short term but after the exam, it'll all be forgotten.

Instead, study for short intervals over a period of time. Students will remember much more for much longer. Why this works is because each time they study and recall the information, their memory for it gets strengthened. The more the study periods of recall then the more they'll remember.

For example, if it's Friday and the test is on Monday then study and recall on Friday afternoon. On Saturday morning, study and recall again. Do this again on Saturday night, Sunday morning, Sunday night and Monday morning. Each study period would be around 20 minutes - depending on how much information there is. By Sunday the recall periods will get shorter and shorter as children will have memorised most of it and the retrieval will be much quicker - maybe 10 minutes at the most.

3. Interleave the Subjects
This depends on how many subjects students have to study. If there are two subjects then spend some time studying one subject, pause and study another subject then return to the first subject. If there are three then interleave the three subjects. What this does is that the more children interleave then the more they'll come back to the topic and the more often they'll recall what they've learnt.

For example, study the test subject for 20 minutes then study another subject or do homework for another 20 minutes.
Take a break or study another subject for 20 minutes. Come back and study the first subject for another 20 minutes, trying to recall the information and so on.

Notice that all these three points are about recalling information from long term memory.

Listening to and Memorising the Quran Increases Memory Ability

As Muslims, we all know the benefits of listening to and memorising the Quran. In this world, we can find a comfort and a cure: Allah ﷻ says in the Quran, *'We send down the Quran as a healing and mercy for the believers...'* (17:82) and guidance *'...It is a guide and a healing to the believers...'* (41:44), among other things. In the Hereafter, we can attain a higher status in Jannah according to what we've memorised. Abdullah ibn Amr reported: The Prophet, peace and blessings be upon him, said, "It will be said to the companion of the Quran: Recite and ascend as you recited in the world. Verily, your rank is determined by the last verse you recite." (al-Tirmidhī)

Research has only recently confirmed the benefits of listening and memorising the Quran. For example, a study found that listening to the Quran can contribute to a calming state of mind in adults (Kamal, Mahmood & Zakaria, 2013), and even premature babies' **vital signs increased** when the Quran is played in another study (Qolizadeh, Myaneh & Rashvand, 2019). As Allah ﷻ says in the Quran that *'Surely in the remembrance of Allah do hearts find comfort.'* (13:28).

These benefits are all well and good but here we are interested in the ability to learn and memorise more. So what does the research say about that? Both the research into just listening to the Quran and memorising the Quran can help improve memorisation. Studies on the effects of just listening to the Quran yielded positive results for improvement of memory in 12 year old female students (Hojjati, Rahimi, Farehani, Sobhi-Gharamaleki, Alian, 2014), and in young 19 to 22 year old adults (Suteja Putra, Gumilar, Rahma Kusuma, Purnomo, & Basumerda, 2018). Studies into Quran memorisation of high school students in Turkey showed improvements in verbal and visual memory, attention speed, and phonemic and semantic fluency (Sirin, Metin, Tarhan, 2021). These students were tested before and after they enrolled in a Quran memorisation program. Adults who had memorised the Quran, known as 'hafiz', also had better memory (Al-Atas, 2011). In fact, college and university students who became hafidh had improved and enhanced academic achievement (Jahangir & Nawaz, 2013).

What this points to is that if you want your child to have better memory for learning then start with the Quran.

The Ability to Memorise the Quran
Everyone has the ability to memorise the Quran. This is one of its miracles. From toddlers to old people, Allah ﷻ has made the Quran easy to memorise. However, some will find it easier to memorise than others. This will depend on a number of factors that can influence the ability to memorise the Quran. The most important are the type of memory processing being used and the motivation. The other factors such as discipline, innate memory strength, iman, age, adab, dua, rhythm and having the same copy of the Quran, may facilitate the process (Dzulkifli, Abdul Rahman, Hussain Solihu, Bashier Badi, Afzal, 2014)

Memory processing is how a person goes about memorising the Quran. There are two types of long term memory processing: maintenance rehearsal and elaboration rehearsal. Maintenance rehearsal is where there is passive repetition with no reference to meaning and associations being made. Elaboration rehearsal is where there is active repetition with meaning and linking to material from long term memory.

The memory processing that is most effective to memorising the Quran is the maintenance rehearsal. This is the miracle of the Quran that anyone can memorise it, even non-Arab speakers who don't understand the meaning of what is being memorised. Allah ﷻ says in the Quran, *'And We have certainly made the Quran easy to remember. So is there anyone who will be mindful?'* (54:17)

What this also means to children is to motivate them to learn. Make it fun. Make it motivating. Make them want to memorise the Quran. The other part is to repeat an ayat or surah over and over again. Children will easily memorise the Quran by listening to it and reciting it repeatedly.

It is much better of course if we understood what Allah ﷻ is telling us (and that is why it is best to learn Arabic) but to preserve the Quran we just need people of hafidh who have committed it to memory.

The other factors mentioned above can also help with memorising the Quran. Discipline is to have the self-discipline to practice the memorisation consistently; to follow the set routine and have the goal in sight. This may sound hard for young children but young children love routines. They might not be able to sit still for long periods of memorisation but if you set up a routine of every morning doing a little bit then this will develop their habit of memorising every morning. As they get older you can increase the time they spent on memorisation.

Innate memory strength is what we're born with. There's not much we can do here but if you noticed that your young children have a good memory then encourage them to start memorising the Quran. Having iman will motivate a person to memorise the Quran as much as they can. Teach your children about Allah ﷻ to nurture their iman. Age plays a part because the younger we are then the easier it is to copy and memorise. Start your children memorising the Quran as early as possible. Adab is the manner in which you approach memorising the Quran. The scholars have given us a set of guidelines that we should follow. There are briefly: wudu, making dua, facing the qiblah, and so on. Listening and then reciting in a familiar rhythm can trigger memory for the sequence of words. Finally, having the same copy of the Quran helps because our memory also relies on the images that we see so to have a consistent image of what we're memorising will help.

Once the Quran is committed to memory, though, it needs to be maintained through continual daily practice and revision. Abdullah ibn Umar reported: The Messenger ﷺ of Allah ﷻ, peace and blessings be upon him, said, "Verily, the parable of the companion of the Quran is that of a tied camel. If he is committed to it, he will keep it. If he releases it, he will lose it." (Al Bukhari & Muslim) This is where maintenance rehearsal is most effective as well.

Ways of Memorising the Quran

There is a study of four popular methods of teaching Quran memorisation (Dzulkifli & Solihu, 2018). It goes into details of the steps in each method. What could be taken from it is the similarities.

1. Each starts with learning new verses by listening to the teacher's pronunciation and repeating exactly what the teacher recited. This is done over and over until the teacher is satisfied that the student has recited it correctly. Remember in Figure 1, this is encoding to get it into long term memory.
2. The next step is the rote memorisation of the new verses. In other words, using maintenance rehearsal. This could take up to four

hours a day in one sitting. This is rehearsal in Figure 1, to use it and practice it from long term memory.
3. The step after this is to revise the old verses that has already been committed to memory with the teacher or a peer listening and correcting any mistakes. This is retrieval in Figure 1, to recall it from long term memory. Without consistently doing these last two steps, whatever was memorised will be forgotten and disappear from long term memory.

Benefit of Understanding the Quran

There are many Muslims who have memorised the Quran. This is important for the preservation of the Quran. However, the ummah needs a lot more Muslims who understands the Quran. We need to understand what Allah ﷻ tells us in the Quran so that we can put it into practice. This is where the tafsir of the Quran plays an important part.

One way to understand the Quran is to reflect on the meaning of the verses. There are many ways we can do this. One way is to attend tafsir classes. We can do **Quran Journaling** :
(http://www.ilmaeducation.com/search/label/Quran)
or even Quran Art Journaling :
(http://www.ilmaeducation.com/2021/02/quran-art-journaling-about-allahs-signs.html).
These are creative ways to introduce children to reflect on the Quran. Download the free templates to start Quran journaling.

The other way to understand the Quran is to understand Arabic. Enroll yourself and your children into Arabic classes. Young children learn languages easily so it's never too early to start.

References

Al-Atas, R. (2011). The Qur'an and memory: a study of the effect of religiosity and memorizing Qur'an as a factor on memory. *Alzheimer's & Dementia,* 7(45), S641-S641. https://doi.org/10.1016/j.jalz.2011.05.1838

Dzulkifli, M. A., Abdul Rahman, A. W., Hussain Solihu, A. K., Bashier Badi, J. A. & Afzal, S. (2014). "Optimizing human memory: An insight from the study of Al Huffaz," *The 5th International Conference on Information and Communication Technology for The Muslim World (ICT4M)*, p1-4, doi: 10.1109/ICT4M.2014.7020624.

Dzulkifli, M. A., & Solihu, A. K. H. (2018). Methods of Qur'ānic Memorisation (Ḥifẓ): Implications for Learning Performance. *Intellectual Discourse, 26*(2), 931–947. Retrieved from https://journals.iium.edu.my/intdiscourse/index.php/id/article/view/1238

Hojjati, A., Rahimi, A., Farehani, M.D., Sobhi-Gharamaleki, N., & Alian, B. (2014). Effectiveness of Quran Tune on memory in children. *Procedia - Social and Behavioral Sciences*, 114, 283 – 286. doi: 10.1016/j.sbspro.2013.12.699

Hudmon, A. (2006). *Learning and Memory*. Chelsea House Publishers.

Jahangir, S.F., & Nawaz, N. (2013). Effects of memorizing Quran by heart (hifz) on later academic achievement. *Journal of Muslim Mental Health, 8*(2), http://dx.doi.org/10.3998/jmmh.10381607.0008.208

Kamal, N.F., Mahmood, N.H., & Zakaria, N.A. (2013). Modeling brain activities during reading working memory task: Comparison between reciting Quran and reading book. *Procedia - Social and Behavioral Sciences*, 97, 83 – 89. doi: 10.1016/j.sbspro.2013.10.207

Qolizadeh, A., Myaneh, Z.T., & Rashvand, F. (2019). Investigating the effect of listening to the Holy Quran on the physiological responses of neonates admitted to neonatal intensive care units: A pilot study. *Advances in Integrative Medicine,* 1-4. https://doi.org/10.1016/j.aimed.2018.08.004

Sirin, S., Metin, B., & Tarhan, N. (2021). The Effect of Memorizing the Quran on Cognitive Functions. *The Journal of Neurobehavioral Sciences, 8*(1), 22-27. DOI: 10.4103/jnbs.jnbs_42_20

CHAPTER 2
Motivation for Mathematical Learning

Aishah Ho

Throughout history, acquiring knowledge of mathematics was highly regarded. Historical figures were not only mathematicians but they were scientists as well. In fact, Muslims mathematicians were polymaths in various fields. In contrast, learning mathematics nowadays has become a caricature of a nerdy intellectual who is disconnected from popular members of society. The subject is no longer compulsory in school. Little emphasis is placed on critical thinking and logic, instead it focuses on life skills.

In order to help our children learn mathematics successfully in school, we must understand that mathematics achievement depends on three factors - emotional and motivational skills and cognitive ability. Starting at an early age, we can help our children to develop foundational mathematic skills and nurture a positive outlook in learning the subject which will sustain their motivation to learn math at high school level and perhaps into their adult life.

Math Anxiety

We all heard the saying of negative thought of failure leads to actual failure. For mathematic, a person's anxiety is caused by his or her perceived ability to complete a mathematical task. Math anxiety is shown to affect a person's ability to learn math (Buckley, S, 2013). There are three causes of math anxiety, namely parents, the environment and teachers (Whyte and Anthony, 2012). As parents, we should stop making negative comments about mathematics. By saying, I'm not good at math or I don't like math, our children will internalise these comments and will produce the same responses when they face difficulty in their learning. Furthermore, when our children make mistakes in their calculation, we must not criticise it. By criticising the mistake, the child equates this to his or her lack of ability in learning math which then feeds into his or her math anxiety.

In terms of the school environment, children learn to hate math from their peers who in turn are influenced by their parents. We can lessen their peers' negative influences by inoculating our children to see math as something amazing in Allah's creations.

Motivation for Math

There are two ways that math can be made more interesting for Muslim children. One is to look at mathematic signs in Allah ﷻ's creations and the other is to study past Muslim mathematicians' contribution to the field of mathematics.

The Signs of Allah ﷻ in Mathematical Patterns

As Muslims, the ultimate purpose of learning mathematics is to see the patterns of Allah ﷻ's creations. Thereby increasing our iman because they are the proofs of His existence. For instance, in the Quran, surah Al-Jathiyah (45), ayah 3:

Indeed, within the heavens and earth are signs for the believers.

Allah ﷻ says in *surah Al-Imran (3), ayah 190*:

Indeed, in the creation of the heavens and the earth and the alternation of the night and the day are signs for those of understanding.

The Arabic word for signs is *ayah*. However, *ayah* has various meanings one of which is a law or a rule. The rule dictates that the moon and the sun following each other but neither one can outstrip the other.

The following two verses speak about Allah ﷻ's command: *surah Al*

A'raf (7), ayah 54:

Indeed, your Lord is Allah, who created the heavens and earth in six days and then established Himself above the Throne. He covers the night with the day, [another night] chasing it rapidly; and [He created] the sun, th

moon, and the stars, subjected by His command. Unquestionably, His is the creation and the command; blessed is Allah, Lord of the worlds.

Surah Al Tala (65), ayah 12:

It is Allah who has created seven heavens and of the earth, the like of them. [His] command descends among them so you may know that Allah is over all things competent and that Allah has encompassed all things in knowledge.

As can be seen from the two verses, His command means that Allah ﷻ has decreed on all created things to follow the laws that govern their functioning. By discovering these laws, in other words, the patterns that created things generate, we come to discover Allah ﷻ.

The most famous pattern found in the natural world and the universe is the *Fibonacci numbers* and by extension the *golden ratio*. The Fibonacci numbers are produced by adding the two preceding numbers to get the next number in the pattern, that is, 1, 1, 2, 3, 5, 8, 13, 21, 34 and so forth. The pattern of growth by living things such as a plant's leaves, a flower's petals, a tree's branches and roots all formed according to the Fibonacci numbers. The golden ratio is simply taking any number in Fibonacci number (the higher number the better) and divide it by the number before it. The answer is approximately 1.618, this number is known as *phi*. This golden ratio produces a spiral formation which can be found in the pineapple eyes, a conifer cone, the sunflower seeds, a nautilus shell, the eye of a hurricane, spiral galaxies and so much more.

Apart from the Fibonacci numbers and the spiral formation in the world and the universe, we can also find these patterns in the human body. For example, the cochlea of the ear, the umbilical cord and the DNA, all follow the spiral formation. The nervous system in fact, for someone who has the 'ideal' face, this means the proportional distance between the eyes, ears, nose and mouth is equal to phi. The book Master Fibonacci: The Man Who Changed Math (Allen, 2019) contains many examples of the relationship between the human body and Fibonacci numbers.

This brings to mind the ayah 53 from surah Al-Fussilat:

We will show them Our signs in the horizons and within themselves until it becomes clear to them that it is the truth. But is it not sufficient concerning your Lord that He is, over all things, a Witness?

There are many videos on the internet which demonstrate the Fibonacci numbers in nature. As parents we can watch these videos with our young children. While watching these videos, we can discuss how all of Allah ﷻ's creations point to His Oneness like an artist when he paints a picture, he embeds his signature in the painting. Similarly, Allah ﷻ's signature can be seen when we look closely and examine the patterns in ourselves, in nature and the universe. When we connect mathematics to discovering Allah ﷻ, our children will see the relevancy of learning math which will sustain their motivation in learning high school math.

Muslim Mathematicians

We can further sustain our children's motivation in learning maths through exploring the contributions of Muslims to the field of mathematics.

For example, all ancient civilisations have different ways to represent a fraction. However it was Abu Bakr Al Hassar from Morocco in the 12th century C.E. that introduced the fraction bar in writing fraction. The fraction bar can be written horizontally or at a slant. Leonardo Fibonacci in the 13th century C.E. then adopted this method of writing fractions which then became the standard for representing fractions (see https://muslimheritage.com/people/scholars/abu-bakr-al-hassar/). It is worth noting that Abu Bakr Al Hassar specialised in the Islamic inheritance laws. Due to his field of work, he invented the way we write fractions today.

It is within the last decade that schools are recognising the contribution of Muslims to the number system. Students are taught the way we write our numbers in the west are based on the Hindu-Arabic numeral system.

However, the emphasis is on the Indian who invented the numeral system while the Muslims were just transmitter of this system to the West. In fact, Muslim mathematicians not only transmitted Indian mathematics but they developed concepts such as polynomial algebra, number theory, combinatorial analysis, numerical analysis, numerical equations, and the geometric construction of equations (Rashed, 1994).

The following is an example of these renown Muslim polymaths (see *https://mathshistory.st-andrews.ac.uk/Biographies/category-arabs/* **for** details).

In the field of algebra, the name Abu Ja'far Muhammad ibn Musa Al-Khwarizmi in the 8th century comes to mind. He wrote comprehensively on algebra with detailed and systematic steps to solving for the unknown. The word algebra came from the title of his book while the word algorithm came from his last name. Al-Khwarizmi wrote this book to solve real life problems in a Muslim's daily life.

In the field of calculus, Ibn al Haytham in the 10th century wrote the formula for finding the sum of the fourth power. This formula, subsequently became a general formula to find the sum of any integral powers. He used integration to calculate the volume of a paraboloid (Katz, 1995). Another notable name to know is Sharaf al-Din al-Tusi in the 12th century. He introduced the idea of a function, and the maxima and minima of a curve. He developed a method to determine whether a cubic equation would have two, one or no solutions.

In the field of trigonometry, Abu Rayhan Biruni in the 11th century, developed the method of triangulation to measure the size of the earth and the distances between various places known as surveyance. In our modern world, the method of triangulation is used by mobile phones to locate where you are as well as by law enforcement to solve crime scenes. Nasir al-Din al-Tusi in the 13th century, created trigonometry as a mathematical discipline in its own right, independent from astronomy. He wrote extensively on spherical trigonometry and the famous *sine law* for plane triangles that we learn in high school $\frac{a}{\sin A} = \frac{b}{\sin B} = \frac{c}{\sin C}$ was written by him.

Cognitive Ability

To achieve mathematic skills we need to have the cognitive ability. A child's math ability is inborn. We cannot make them into a genius but we can help them to achieve a level of success in their learning mathematics.

The most important skill a child can develop at an early age is to be able to identify patterns. If we reduce all the topics of mathematics, we will find a commonality between them all and that is about identifying patterns. The focus of primary school mathematics is finding patterns. As students move into high schools, the first two years or so, they are taught how to represent the observed pattern as a mathematical equation and also as a graph. The purpose of writing mathematical equations is to be able to make prediction. This whole process comes under the topic of algebra. We know that life is not static. Everything in the universe is always in a state of changes. In order to represent these changes, students are then taught calculus. Calculus is basically the study of the rate of changes, in other words, how can we represent the changes in our life, in the world and in the universe as an equation? There are other topics taught in school, one of which is Geometry. Geometry is usually connected with developing inductive and deductive logic. This is in essence the objectives of learning math in school.

As can be seen, it is very important to help our children to develop the ability to see patterns in everyday life. An example of children learning pattern at an early age is to count from 1 to 10. Children will recognise that two will always follow after 1, three after two and so forth. By extension, they will realise that there is a pattern after ten, in that the cycle of counting repeats with the digits of 1 to 9. Using this pattern, they can apply it to counting from 20 to 50. At an advance level, the children can predict the next even number after 4. This is only possible if they understand the pattern of even numbers.

Understanding the concept of numbers is innate in everyone. It is what Islam called the 'fitrah'. When children learn to count, there are various ways we can help them to develop a strong foundation in learning math. Do activities that connect the symbolic representation of numbers to everyday life and encourage them to say the numbers out loud. For more details on number learning in pre-schoolers, see http://www.ilmaeducation.com/2013/03/learning-numbers.html. Another highly recommended activity is to have children think of all the different ways (by adding only, for more advance level, try subtraction) that we can make numbers from 1 to 10. For example, the number 4. The answers would be 4 + 0, 1 + 3, and 2 + 2. We do the same for 7. The answers would be 7 + 0, 1 + 6, 2 + 5, and 3 + 4. Use a number line to demonstrate the answers. This activity helps children to recognise the patterns between these numbers and prepare them for mental computation.

There are many researches done on finding the predictors of academic achievement. The most cited work is from Duncan et al, (2007) which showed that early childhood academic skills such as mathematics have a profound effect on later academic achievement. There is also a research done on the effect of kindergarten math skills on eight grade achievement in reading, math and science (Claessens and Engel, 2013). In fact, early numeracy skills at the preschool level can predict how well a child will perform mathematics at fifth grade or in Year 5 (Nguyen et al, 2015). This research further identifies counting skills (knowledge of number words and symbols, number word sequence and enumeration) as the strongest influencer on a child math achievement in Year 5. When teaching toddlers to count numbers, they may make mistakes, for example 1, 2, 4, 5. We need to refrain from telling them their mistakes. Instead, we continue modelling the counting sequence again and again. The toddlers will hear and learn to identify the correct sequence. When a child is shamed or criticised for making mistakes, it inhibits his or her learning of a new skill.

There are milestones in a child's math abilities at various stage of development that we can use to help them learn math. For instance, a baby from 0 to 12 months, starts to understand basic cause and effect while a child from age 1 to 2 can see patterns around them, begins to recite numbers and understand that these numbers mean 'how many'. On the other hand, a child from age 3 to 4 can count up to 20 and connect the numeral symbol of 5 to mean five. They start to make simple predictions whereas a five-year-old child can add numbers using his or her fingers. For a comprehensive list, refer to the *article 'Math Skills: What to expect at different ages'* from Amanda Morin's website:

(https://www.understood.org/en/articles/math-skills-what-to-expect-at-different-ages) where she lists the ages from babies to high schoolers.

When it comes to learning mathematics, we need to nurture in our children a positive mindset regarding it. Three of the ways to do this is by:

(1) removing our own negative attitudes and biases towards learning math that can influence the children,

(2) developing motivation in our children to learn math whether it is seeing the patterns in Allah﷾'s creation or learning about Muslim mathematicians, and

(3) developing a strong foundation for number sense at an early age.

Mathematical Activities

Preschool:

1. Count everything. As you live your daily life with your pre-schooler, count out loud everything that you see: count steps as you walk up or down, count cars in a parking lot, count petals on a flower, count cereals and so on. These counting activities will get your children familiar with the number sequence, rote counting and eventually, counting with one-to-one correspondence.
2. Play with number symbols. Use number puzzles, number playdough cutters, number stamps, magnetic numbers, counting books and so on. Let children play with them so they will eventually recognise them. For more details on this, read http://www.ilmaeducation.com/2017/10/5-fun-preschool-number-activities.html
3. Chant number finger rhymes such as Five Little Speckled Frogs, 12345 Once I Caught a Fish Alive, etc. This is a fun way for children to learn the number sequence, rote counting and one-to-one correspondence.

Primary School:

4. Start to relate mathematical concepts like fractions and decimals to real life, for example, cutting a bar of chocolate into half to

share or do a trade in for a dollar coin or a two dollar coin. In other words, children collect five, ten, twenty and fifty cent coins. As soon as their coins add up to 100 or 200, they can swap for the gold coin.
5. Pose problems for the children to solve. For example, the cupcake recipe makes 12 but you only want to make 6 cupcakes. Look at the ingredients and ask them what you should do. Alternatively, while shopping, ask them which is a better buy: a 100g jar of peanut butter or 200g for whatever the price is.

High School:

6. Study the Fibonacci numbers by going outside and observing nature. Study several plants, flowers or trees and observe the number of leaves, petals or branches. Record them down. What do students notice? Do they follow Fibonacci numbers?
7. Similarly, study the golden ratio. Divide a Fibonacci number by the number before it. Do they all equal 1.618? Alternatively, when you have a line and you split this line into two parts such that when you divide the longer part by the shorter part, it is equal to 1.618. To apply this, take the label of a bottle of coca cola. Measure the top of the label to its bottom. At the bottom of the word cola, this is where you will divide the label into two parts. Now divide the top part by the bottom part. Another activity is to calculate the perfect face shape. Take some photos of famous movie stars, divide the length of their faces, from the hairline to the chin, by the widest width of their faces. If it is equal to 1.6 then they have the perfect face shape.

References

Allen, S. (2019). Master Fibonacci: The Man Who Changed Math Paperback. Fibonacci Inc

Buckley, S. (2013). Deconstructing maths anxiety: Helping students to develop a positive attitude towards learning maths. Australian Council for Educational Research.

Claessens,A., Engel, M. (2013). How important is where you start? Early mathematics knowledge and later school success. *Teachers College Record, 115*(6).

Duncan, G. J., Dowsett, C. J., Claessens, A., Magnuson, K., Huston, A. C., Klebanov, P., Pagani, L. S., Feinstein, L., Engel, M., Brooks-Gunn, J., Sexton, H., Duckworth, K., & Japel, C. (2007). School readiness and later achievement. *Developmental Psychology, 43*(6), 1428–1446

Katz, V. J. (1995). Ideas of Calculus in Islam and India. *Mathematics Magazine, 68* (3): 163–74, doi:10.2307/2691411, JSTOR 2691411

Nguyen, T; Watts, T W.; Duncan, G J.; Clements, D H.; Sarama, J; Wolfe, C B., Spitler, M E. (2015). What Specific Preschool Math Skills Predict Later Math Achievement? *Society for Research on Educational Effectiveness*

Rashed, R. (1994). The development of Arabic mathematics: Between arithmetic and algebra. London,

Whyte, J., and ANTHONY, G. (2012). Maths Anxiety: The Fear Factor in the mathematics Classroom. *New Zealand Journal of Teachers' Work, 9*(1), 6-15.

CHAPTER 3
Methodology for Learning Science

Meenara Khan

If learning the truth is the scientist's goal, then he must make himself the enemy of all that he reads. — Ibn Al-Haytham

Learning and teaching are the core components of what developed the first Muslims. Their faith, determination, and trust in a way of life was unlike the society of the Arabian Peninsula. From the first revelations to the innovative advances contributing to the modern world, it was the strive for knowledge and education that pushed human beings to satisfy their curiosity. Scientists like Ibn Sina, Ibn Nafis, Al-Jazari, Al-Khwarizmi, Al-Haytham are examples of the fabulous struggle for knowledge and to solve the problems that faced humanity at their time. Science was a largely explored field where many before them pondered on the systems of nature in front of them and answered the questions posed.

The importance of knowledge, *ilm* (علم), is evident by the first revelation, where Allah ﷻ commanded the Prophet Muhammad ﷺ and all humans:

1. اقْرَأْ بِاسْمِ رَبِّكَ الَّذِى خَلَقَ

2. خَلَقَ الْإِنسَٰنَ مِنْ عَلَقٍ

3. اقْرَأْ وَرَبُّكَ الْأَكْرَمُ

4. الَّذِى عَلَّمَ بِالْقَلَمِ

5. عَلَّمَ الْإِنسَٰنَ مَا لَمْ يَعْلَمْ

"Read. "Read in the name of thy Lord who created; [He] created the human being from blood clot. Read in the name of thy Lord who taught by

the pen: [He] taught the human being what he did not know." (96:1-5).[32]

Note from the verses how reading is the most important way to collect information. Reading is an important skill for gathering information, developing the mind, and making sense of words. Before anyone can question anything, they must have evidence and facts to make a judgement from in order to come up with ways to prove or discredit the claim. This becomes an important part of the scientific method where observation involves intense research by reading, collecting data, and observing the actual phenomena.

Remember the story of Ibrahim عليه السلام and how he was searching for God? Ibrahim عليه السلام saw how the people in his town created idols and worshipped the sky. Allah ﷻ gave Ibrahim عليه السلام wisdom, which made Ibrahim عليه السلام question the people, even his own father, who sculpted these idols. To discover the truth, Ibrahim عليه السلام spent nights observing the sky and thinking about who could be the one and only Creator. Here, we see how observing and thinking were qualities of our Prophets (May Allah be pleased with them all). Through observations and questioning, similar to the modern scientific method, Ibrahim عليه السلام was able to conclude that Allah ﷻ was the only Creator.

Ibrahim عليه السلام's experience is mentioned by Allah ﷻ as:

وَكَذَٰلِكَ نُرِىٓ إِبْرَٰهِيمَ مَلَكُوتَ ٱلسَّمَٰوَٰتِ وَٱلْأَرْضِ وَلِيَكُونَ مِنَ ٱلْمُوقِنِينَ

فَلَمَّا جَنَّ عَلَيْهِ ٱلَّيْلُ رَءَا كَوْكَبًا قَالَ هَٰذَا رَبِّى فَلَمَّآ أَفَلَ قَالَ لَآ أُحِبُّ ٱلْءَافِلِينَ

فَلَمَّا رَءَا ٱلْقَمَرَ بَازِغًا قَالَ هَٰذَا رَبِّى فَلَمَّآ أَفَلَ قَالَ لَئِن لَّمْ يَهْدِنِى رَبِّى لَأَكُونَنَّ مِنَ ٱلْقَوْمِ ٱلضَّآلِّينَ

فَلَمَّا رَءَا ٱلشَّمْسَ بَازِغَةً قَالَ هَٰذَا رَبِّى هَٰذَآ أَكْبَرُ فَلَمَّآ أَفَلَتْ قَالَ يَٰقَوْمِ إِنِّى بَرِىٓءٌ مِّمَّا تُشْرِكُونَ

إِنِّى وَجَّهْتُ وَجْهِىَ لِلَّذِى فَطَرَ ٱلسَّمَٰوَٰتِ وَٱلْأَرْضَ حَنِيفًا وَمَآ أَنَا۠ مِنَ ٱلْمُشْرِكِينَ

"And thus did We show Abraham the realm of the heavens and the earth that he would be among the certain [in faith]."

"So when the night covered him [with darkness], he saw a star. He said, "This is my lord." But when it set, he said, "I like not those that set [i.e., disappear]."

"And when he saw the moon rising, he said, "This is my lord." But when it set, he said, "Unless my Lord guides me, I will surely be among the people gone astray."

"And when he saw the sun rising, he said, "This is my lord; this is greater." But when it set, he said, "O my people, indeed I am free from what you associate with Allah."

"Indeed, I have turned my face [i.e., self] toward He who created the heavens and the earth, inclining toward truth, and I am not of those who associate others with Allah." (6:75-79) [32]

The scientific method is a process of collecting data by observations, questioning, thinking, and utilizing previous knowledge. A collection of numerical and observational data supports or refutes a claim. Certain tests are performed, or various experiments are conducted with multiple trials to see the causes and effects. If things don't work out, you adjust the investigation by changing factors, like temperature, time, measurement, etc., to see if it affects the experiment. Finally, you conduct a thorough data collection and make a conclusion about the results. Allah ﷻ says:

فِى خَلْقِ ٱلسَّمَٰوَٰتِ وَٱلْأَرْضِ وَٱخْتِلَٰفِ ٱلَّيْلِ وَٱلنَّهَارِ لَءَايَٰتٍ لِّأُو۟لِى ٱلْأَلْبَٰبِ

"Look! In the creation of the heavens and the earth and (in) the difference of night and day are tokens (of His sovereignty) for men of understanding." (3:190) [32]

We see that Allah ﷻ is commanding the believers to look at their surroundings, to explore and make sense of the physical world, and connect with their Creator. This evidence shows that the scientific method is found in the early Islamic sources and clearly describes how humans should search for information.

Islam Requires People to Reflect

"I adore and respect whatever encourages me to think, and I definitely found that element in the Qur'an... I was always taken by verses in the Qur'an which ask people to ponder the universe." — Rim al Turkmani

In Arabic, *Tafakur* (تَفَكُّر) means to contemplate, ponder, reflect, and think deeply. The word for "intellect" is *'Aql* (عقل), meaning sense, reason, understanding, comprehension, rationality, and mind. When Islam came and the Quran was revealed, Allah ﷻ required people to contemplate and to think about the existence of life. Islam instructed people to believe by rational thinking, not blind following, and required people to think and reflect on their intentions. Allah ﷻ says:

وَإِذَا قِيلَ لَهُمُ ٱتَّبِعُوا۟ مَآ أَنزَلَ ٱللَّهُ قَالُوا۟ بَلْ نَتَّبِعُ مَآ أَلْفَيْنَا عَلَيْهِ ءَابَآءَنَآۚ أَوَلَوْ كَانَ ءَابَآؤُهُمْ لَا يَعْقِلُونَ شَيْـًٔا وَلَا يَهْتَدُونَ

"And when it is said to them: 'Follow that which Allah has revealed,' they say: 'We follow that wherein we found our fathers.' What! Even though their fathers were wholly unintelligent and devoid of guidance!" (2:170)[32]

Allah ﷻ also said:

أَوَلَمْ يَتَفَكَّرُوا۟ فِىٓ أَنفُسِهِمۗ مَّا خَلَقَ ٱللَّهُ ٱلسَّمَٰوَٰتِ وَٱلْأَرْضَ وَمَا بَيْنَهُمَآ إِلَّا بِٱلْحَقِّ وَأَجَلٍ مُّسَمًّىۗ وَإِنَّ كَثِيرًا مِّنَ ٱلنَّاسِ بِلِقَآئِ رَبِّهِمْ لَكَٰفِرُونَ

Do they not contemplate within themselves? Allah has not created the heavens and the earth and what is between them except in truth and for a specified term. And indeed, many of the people, in [the matter of] the meeting with their Lord, are disbelievers. (30:8) [32]

Abu Darda رضي الله عنه also reported that the Messenger of Allah ﷺ said:

Verily, the angels lower their wings for the seeker of knowledge. The inhabitants of the heavens and earth, even the fish in the depths of the water, seek forgiveness for the scholar. The virtue of the scholar over the worshiper is like the superiority of the moon over the stars. The scholars are the inheritors of the Prophets. They do not leave behind gold or silver coins, but rather they leave behind knowledge. Whoever has taken hold of it has been given an abundant share. **(Sunan Abī Dāwūd 3641)**[33]

This hadith shows the honor and importance of those who have sought knowledge and the one who shares the knowledge. From this, we can also see how the scientists and scholars of the Muslim civilization received the importance and attention of the Caliphs and Sultans at the time. Allah ﷻ says:

إِنَّ فِى خَلْقِ ٱلسَّمَٰوَٰتِ وَٱلْأَرْضِ وَٱخْتِلَٰفِ ٱلَّيْلِ وَٱلنَّهَارِ وَٱلْفُلْكِ ٱلَّتِى تَجْرِى فِى ٱلْبَحْرِ بِمَا يَنفَعُ ٱلنَّاسَ وَمَا أَنزَلَ ٱللَّهُ مِنَ ٱلسَّمَآءِ مِن مَّآءٍ فَأَحْيَا بِهِ ٱلْأَرْضَ بَعْدَ مَوْتِهَا وَبَثَّ فِيهَا مِن كُلِّ دَآبَّةٍ وَتَصْرِيفِ ٱلرِّيَٰحِ وَٱلسَّحَابِ ٱلْمُسَخَّرِ بَيْنَ ٱلسَّمَآءِ وَٱلْأَرْضِ لَءَايَٰتٍ لِّقَوْمٍ يَعْقِلُونَ

"Lo in the creation of the heavens and the earth and the difference of night and day and the ships which run upon the sea with that which is of use to men, and the water which Allah sends down from the sky thereby reviving the earth after its death and dispersing all kinds of beasts therein, and in the ordinance of the winds and the clouds obedient between heaven and earth, these are signs for people who have sense." (2:164) [32]

And finally, not knowing or refusing to ask questions or to learn about something is not an excuse. Jabir رضي الله عنه reported that the Messenger of Allah ﷺ said:

إِنَّمَا شِفَاءُ الْعِيِّ السُّؤَالُ

Verily, the only cure for ignorance is to ask questions. (Sunan Abī Dāwūd 336)[33]

Methodologies For Learning Science

The most important aspect of teaching is to make it engaging and revolve around the curiosity of the students. There are many ways to make learning opportunities fun for all learners. Science is all around us and can be seen in daily activities. When we cook, we see chemistry. When we plant in our garden, we see biology. When we play outside or ride our bikes, we see physics. These are great learning experiences where children can see the laws of nature in action. Allah ﷻ says in the Holy Quran:

فَهَلْ يَنظُرُونَ إِلَّا سُنَّتَ ٱلْأَوَّلِينَ ۚ فَلَن تَجِدَ لِسُنَّتِ ٱللَّهِ تَبْدِيلًا ۖ وَلَن تَجِدَ لِسُنَّتِ ٱللَّهِ تَحْوِيلًا

"Then should they wait for aught except the way of former people? For you shall not find any alteration in the course of Allah." (35:43) [32]

Starting Everyone From The Same Page

Many of us have heard about the Flat Earth theory while others are sure that the Earth is a sphere. This shows that most students don't come into a classroom with the same thinking or knowledge. In fact, students come with many misconceptions. A misconception is defined as inaccurate or incomplete ideas about a concept. A skillful teacher should begin a topic with the basics, starting from scratch to bring all students on one platform. Therefore, it is crucial to help students share their ideas and to clear up misunderstandings. This makes learning the material easier and doesn't limit a students' ability to grow cognitively. [31]

LEARNING SCIENCE: A HANDS-ON APPROACH

Also known as student-centered classrooms, research has shown that hands-on, active learning-based lessons and classrooms help students learn better and are more engaging than traditional, teacher-centered, lecture only lessons and classrooms. Hands-on learning is the process of learning by experiences and kinesthetics. These experiences include interactions with one's environment such as the people, habitat, nature, and objects. Active learning environments help students to be in control of their learning and discovery. They are not being told what to learn or believe, rather they are actively searching for the facts to support or expose their misconceptions and to grow their knowledge. This helps students to challenge other claims and use evidence to support their ideas and discoveries.

Some of the best ways to teach science is to implement various kinds of learning formats such as: discovery-learning, group activities, scavenger hunts, investigation, project-based learning, etc. Examples include video diaries, inquiry-based learning, experimental investigation, and field trips. These activities help students to build social skills such as task management, communication, negotiation, and collaboration. They also help students to understand how to share their thoughts and use critical thinking skills to solve a problem. Studies show active learning in science that requires productivity and group collaboration is the most successful and beneficial way of teaching science to children. Most experts believe that the best way for teaching anything is to have students do it by themselves. This is very beneficial for children who are kinesthetic learners, as they learn by using their senses and have visual demonstrations for support.

Discovery Learning

Discovery learning is a hands-on method developed by Jerome Bruner, who believed that everyone should learn by doing. This kind of learning requires students to acquire information and facts by initially interacting with their environment or objects. They can be prompted to ask questions, make observations, hypothesize, ponder, etc. This helps the student to make actual discoveries about a topic rather than conduct traditional, step wise experiments that give concrete instructions on what to do and the expected results they will see. Students are then evaluated for a summary of what they did rather than what they saw, which is not the purpose of discovery-based learning. Students are evaluated based on their skills. This type of learning activity is beneficial for students with behavior issues and helps English Language Learner students to practice their communication skills in a group setting.

Scavenger Hunts

Scavenger hunts are another form of hands-on, organized activities. These activities are guided by a topic and a series of clues or prompts that make students relate their learning to the real world. Students go "hunting" for the answers while they learn or make inferences about the topic. Students develop important skill sets such as: critical thinking and analysis, questioning, collaboration, meticulous and precision problem-solving, and other skills that create the modern science student. It is very easy to customize these scavenger hunts to all grade levels and student abilities, and even make thematic scavenger hunts to create more engagement. Students pretend to behave like detectives, searching for clues and answers while they are going through a process of learning and discovery.[33]

Inquiry Based Learning

Inquiry based learning is a learning technique that is used to help learners come up with their own definitions and theories about a concept. In this setting, students are given a problem or question. They are instructed to investigate the problem through reading, observations, and discussions about the concept. Students use materials to understand the concept and to collect data. Finally, they come up with their own discoveries and explanations about the concept. The teacher acts as the facilitator who makes sure that students are following the behavior and classroom expectations while staying on task. The teacher may even help students understand and use critical thinking and analysis skills to develop their conceptual understanding. Then the class discusses what they did and the lesson closes with a well-rounded understanding of the concept.

Peer Instruction

Peer instruction is a teaching strategy where students teach each other concepts and ideas and the teacher themselves are facilitators of the lesson. Rather than covering a topic from the textbook, teachers present the material through short presentations addressing the main points of the topic, but the lesson dedicates most of the time to student engagement and interaction. Afterwards, students answer short questions about the topic. If students respond poorly to the questions, there is another discussion of the main points. But if students answer correctly, the class moves on to having the students discuss with each other about their answers and to find another student who has a different answer from them, and to discuss the reasons for their answers with their peers. This is the important aspect of the strategy as students must convince their peers to understand the concept through their own understanding. Only then are all students on the same platform of conceptual understanding and the results of their assessment reflect whether all students were able to answer questions correctly. The final discussion is made around clarifying and correcting the concepts of all students. This strategy ensures all students participate in the class discussion compared to the few students who participate majority of the time. This helps the teacher to get feedback about student performance, even intervene and take remedial action if they feel necessary. This type of assessment for learning without waiting until formative assessments are conducted, which is usually when teachers see that there is a gap in learning and weak basic skills, allows for teachers to use summative assessment techniques so all students come up to the same level of expectation and learning. A study conducted in Nigerian schools about peer instruction used the Peer Instruction approach coupled with a ConcepTest method to question students every so often to check their understanding and learning.[17]

Lecture Based Instruction

Lecture based teaching is the most common teaching method that is teacher-centered. This traditional method is not only ineffective, but it doesn't help build curiosity nor does it increase the scientific characteristics of science students. A study conducted in secondary schools in rural Khairpur, Pakistan confirmed that the majority of teachers used only lecture based teaching methods that didn't meet the demands of the modern science student and did not help students learn important scientific and critical thinking skills. Since the methodology is solely dependent on the teacher, it is important to note that undertrained and unqualified teachers impact the ability of student learning. The study concluded that many factors contributed to low engagement in secondary science education. These factors included outdated information in textbooks, little to no science activities or demonstrations, no student involvement or participation, extension activities, field experiences, lack of resources, and unprofessional and inexperienced teachers. It is imperative that teachers must be highly qualified and skilled in their discipline. Teachers should rely on other resources besides the textbook to give students a beneficial science education experience.[12]

Utilizing The Brain's Remarkable Abilities

Multiple intelligence is the idea that a person has different kinds of intellectual capabilities, strengths, and weaknesses of how they learn, and they can learn knowledge in multiple ways. According to its founder, Howard Gardner believes that every human being has multiple intelligence and abilities to learn. Gardner says that intelligence is a biopsychological trait that organisms have so they can understand and process their surroundings in different ways. This means that each person may understand things when associating themselves more with a specific setting or technique that allows them to learn and absorb the information more efficiently. There are different kinds of multiple intelligences:

1. Verbal-linguistic intelligence (well-developed verbal skills and sensitivity to the sounds, meanings, and rhythms of words)

2. Logical-mathematical intelligence (ability to think conceptually and abstractly, and capacity to discern logical and numerical patterns)

3. Spatial-visual intelligence (capacity to think in images and pictures, to visualize accurately and abstractly)
4. Bodily-kinesthetic intelligence (ability to control one's body movements and to handle objects skillfully)
5. Musical intelligences (ability to produce and appreciate rhythm, pitch, and timber)
6. Interpersonal intelligence (capacity to detect and respond appropriately to the moods, motivations, and desires of others)
7. Intrapersonal (capacity to be self-aware and in tune with feelings, values, beliefs and thinking processes)
8. Naturalist intelligence (ability to recognize and categorize plants, animals, and other objects in nature)
9. Existential intelligence (sensitivity and capacity to tackle deep questions about human existence such as, "What is the meaning of life? Why do we die? How did we get here?")

This means that learning materials should be presented in multiple ways. An example would be that if a teacher is teaching about apples, the concept of the apple should be presented in multiple ways. The chart below describes an example of how an apple can be taught using the Multiple Intelligence theory:

Table 1. Example of Using Multiple Intelligence Theory to Learn

Verbal-linguistic intelligence (well-developed verbal skills and sensitivity to the sounds, meanings, and rhythms of words)	Describe the apple's appearance, write a poem or summary of the apple
Logical-mathematical intelligence (ability to think conceptually and abstractly, and capacity to discern logical and numerical patterns)	Cut the apple in half through the center to show the pattern or symmetry in the center of the apple. Represent the apple as fractions: pieces eaten compared to total pieces of the apple.
Spatial-visual intelligence (capacity to	Compare the size of the apple to

think in images and pictures, to visualize accurately and abstractly)	other objects
Bodily-kinesthetic intelligence (ability to control one's body movements and to handle objects skillfully)	Carefully slice the apple using a knife, juggle multiple apples, make apple pie
Musical intelligences (ability to produce and appreciate rhythm, pitch, and timber)	Make/write a song about apples
Interpersonal intelligence (capacity to detect and respond appropriately to the moods, motivations, and desires of others)	Giving an apple to someone who is hungry, share your apple with others by cutting it into pieces
Intrapersonal (capacity to be self-aware and in tune with feelings, values, beliefs and thinking processes)	Believing/Convincing others that apples are healthy snacks to eat
Naturalist intelligence (ability to recognize and categorize plants, animals, and other objects in nature)	Study the life cycle of an apple tree, plant an apple tree using seeds from the apple
Existential intelligence (sensitivity and capacity to tackle deep questions about human existence such as, "What is the meaning of life? Why do we die? How did we get here?")	What is the purpose of an apple? Why do we eat apples? How were they created?

The point of multiple intelligences is that those who have learned information in different ways and are knowledgeable about the object, are able to reach more students and learners, making the learning experience more engaging and interesting. The learner can retain the information about the object or concept for a longer period and can further explain it to others using their own learning.

In the Quran, Allah ﷻ has commanded the believers to observe and ponder on His existence. The Quran also describes how humans learn using their intelligence, *Aql* (العقل), and describes multiple intelligence also.

Table 2. The Quran and Multiple Intelligences

Verbal-linguistic intelligence (well-developed verbal skills and sensitivity to the sounds, meanings, and rhythms of words)	(20:28) يَفْقَهُوا قَوْلِى "That they may understand my speech."[32]
Logical-mathematical intelligence (ability to think conceptually and abstractly, and capacity to discern logical and numerical patterns)	مَثَلُ ٱلَّذِينَ يُنفِقُونَ أَمْوَٰلَهُمْ فِى سَبِيلِ ٱللَّهِ كَمَثَلِ حَبَّةٍ أَنۢبَتَتْ سَبْعَ سَنَابِلَ فِى كُلِّ سُنۢبُلَةٍ مِّا۟ئَةُ حَبَّةٍ ۗ وَٱللَّهُ يُضَٰعِفُ لِمَن يَشَآءُ ۗ وَٱللَّهُ وَٰسِعٌ عَلِيمٌ (2:261) "The example of those who spend their wealth in the way of Allah is like a seed [of grain] which grows seven spikes; in each spike is a hundred grains. And Allah multiplies [His reward] for whom He wills. And Allah is all-Encompassing and knowing."[32]
Spatial-visual intelligence (capacity to think in images and pictures, to visualize accurately and abstractly)	وَهُوَ ٱلَّذِى مَدَّ ٱلْأَرْضَ وَجَعَلَ فِيهَا رَوَٰسِىَ وَأَنْهَٰرًۭا ۖ وَمِن كُلِّ ٱلثَّمَرَٰتِ جَعَلَ فِيهَا زَوْجَيْنِ ٱثْنَيْنِ ۖ يُغْشِى ٱلَّيْلَ ٱلنَّهَارَ ۚ إِنَّ فِى ذَٰلِكَ لَءَايَٰتٍۢ لِّقَوْمٍۢ يَتَفَكَّرُونَ (13:3) "And it is He who spread the earth and placed therein firmly set mountains and rivers; and from all of the fruits He made therein two mates; He causes the night to cover the day. Indeed, these are signs for people who give thought."[32]
Bodily-kinesthetic intelligence (ability to control one's body movements and to handle objects skillfully)	فَبَعَثَ ٱللَّهُ غُرَابًۭا يَبْحَثُ فِى ٱلْأَرْضِ لِيُرِيَهُۥ كَيْفَ يُوَٰرِى سَوْءَةَ أَخِيهِ ۚ قَالَ يَٰوَيْلَتَىٰٓ أَعَجَزْتُ أَنْ أَكُونَ مِثْلَ هَٰذَا ٱلْغُرَابِ فَأُوَٰرِىَ سَوْءَةَ أَخِى ۖ فَأَصْبَحَ مِنَ ٱلنَّٰدِمِينَ (5:31) "Thereupon Allah sent forth a raven

	who began to scratch the earth to show him how he might cover the corpse of his brother. So, seeing he cried: 'Woe unto me! Was I unable even to be like this raven and find a way to cover the corpse of my brother? Then he became full of remorse at his doing." [33]
Musical intelligences (ability to produce and appreciate rhythm, pitch and timber)	(73:4) أَوْ زِدْ عَلَيْهِ وَرَتِّلِ ٱلْقُرْءَانَ تَرْتِيلًا "Or add to it, and recite the Qur'ān with measured recitation." [32]
Interpersonal intelligence (capacity to detect and respond appropriately to the moods, motivations and desires of others)	وَإِذْ أَخَذْنَا مِيثَٰقَ بَنِىٓ إِسْرَٰٓءِيلَ لَا تَعْبُدُونَ إِلَّا ٱللَّهَ وَبِٱلْوَٰلِدَيْنِ إِحْسَانًا وَذِى ٱلْقُرْبَىٰ وَٱلْيَتَٰمَىٰ وَٱلْمَسَٰكِينِ وَقُولُوا۟ لِلنَّاسِ حُسْنًا وَأَقِيمُوا۟ ٱلصَّلَوٰةَ وَءَاتُوا۟ ٱلزَّكَوٰةَ ثُمَّ تَوَلَّيْتُمْ إِلَّا قَلِيلًا مِّنكُمْ وَأَنتُم مُّعْرِضُونَ (2:83) "You shall serve none but Allah and do good to parents, kinsmen, orphans and the needy; you shall speak kindly to people and establish Prayer and give zakah." [32]
Intrapersonal (capacity to be self-aware and in tune with inner feelings, values, beliefs and thinking processes)	وَذَا ٱلنُّونِ إِذ ذَّهَبَ مُغَٰضِبًا فَظَنَّ أَن لَّن نَّقْدِرَ عَلَيْهِ فَنَادَىٰ فِى ٱلظُّلُمَٰتِ أَن لَّآ إِلَٰهَ إِلَّآ أَنتَ سُبْحَٰنَكَ إِنِّى كُنتُ مِنَ ٱلظَّٰلِمِينَ (21:87) "There is no deity except You; exalted are You. Indeed, I have been of the wrongdoers." [32]
Naturalist intelligence (ability to recognize and categorize plants, animals and other objects in nature)	ثُمَّ كُلِى مِن كُلِّ ٱلثَّمَرَٰتِ فَٱسْلُكِى سُبُلَ رَبِّكِ ذُلُلًا يَخْرُجُ مِنۢ بُطُونِهَا شَرَابٌ مُّخْتَلِفٌ أَلْوَٰنُهُۥ فِيهِ شِفَآءٌ لِّلنَّاسِ إِنَّ فِى ذَٰلِكَ لَءَايَةً لِّقَوْمٍ يَتَفَكَّرُونَ (16:69) "Then eat of every (kind) of fruit and walk the path of your Lord, which has been facilitated (for you). From the bee's stomach comes a drink

	(honey) of various colors, in which there is healing medicine for humans. Surely in this, there is truly a sign (the greatness of God) for those who think." [32]
Existential intelligence (sensitivity and capacity to tackle deep questions about human existence such as, "What is the meaning of life? Why do we die? How did we get here?"	وَإِذْ قَالَ إِبْرَٰهِۦمُ رَبِّ أَرِنِى كَيْفَ تُحْىِ ٱلْمَوْتَىٰ ۖ قَالَ أَوَلَمْ تُؤْمِن ۖ قَالَ بَلَىٰ وَلَٰكِن لِّيَطْمَئِنَّ قَلْبِى ۖ قَالَ فَخُذْ أَرْبَعَةً مِّنَ ٱلطَّيْرِ فَصُرْهُنَّ إِلَيْكَ ثُمَّ ٱجْعَلْ عَلَىٰ كُلِّ جَبَلٍ مِّنْهُنَّ جُزْءًا ثُمَّ ٱدْعُهُنَّ يَأْتِينَكَ سَعْيًا ۚ وَٱعْلَمْ أَنَّ ٱللَّهَ عَزِيزٌ حَكِيمٌ (2:260) "And [mention] when Abraham said, "My Lord, show me how You give life to the dead." [Allah] said, "Have you not believed?" He said, "Yes, but [I ask] only that my heart may be satisfied." [Allah] said, "Take four birds and commit them to yourself. Then [after slaughtering them] put on each hill a portion of them; then call them - they will come [flying] to you in haste. And know that Allah is Exalted in Might and Wise." [32]

Science From An Islamic Perspective

سَنُرِيهِمْ ءَايَٰتِنَا فِى ٱلْءَافَاقِ وَفِىٓ أَنفُسِهِمْ حَتَّىٰ يَتَبَيَّنَ لَهُمْ أَنَّهُ ٱلْحَقُّ ۗ أَوَلَمْ يَكْفِ بِرَبِّكَ أَنَّهُۥ عَلَىٰ كُلِّ شَىْءٍ شَهِيدٌ

"We (Allah) will show you (mankind) our signs/patterns in the horizons/universe and in yourselves until you are convinced that the revelation is the truth." (14:53) [32]

When you think about science today, how do you feel about it? Does your perspective about science change when you view it as a Muslim? Do you feel contradicted or empowered? Contrary to some beliefs, it is imperative to note that Islam never denied science. There is a popular argument that religion hinders material and scientific progress. This is based on the historical fact that in the Dark ages of Europe, scientists and thinkers of that time were criticized and seen as opponents of the Church. The reason for the separation of church and state was because of the inability of the Church to meet the needs and problems of their citizens at the time and it didn't allow scientists and thinkers to propose their ideas and innovations. It was unable to solve the issue of disunity, poverty, and rather caused oppression among the society, especially towards the people who didn't agree with the Church. As a result, the Church had to reform itself if it were to survive in Europe leading to the European Reformation period. Even then, the Church was unable to continue its ruling and was restricted in its authority to just spiritual rituals and morals.[26]

We can see that because the Church didn't support or appreciate the scientists and thinkers, European scientific advancement stagnated while the Muslim empires were at their zenith in scientific and technological advancements. Rather, we see that Islam was a driving force behind the innovations of the Islamic Golden age. A crucial fact about Islam is that it is not just a religion but a way of life. Since Islam is a way of life, that means that it has systems in place that govern every aspect of human life. It helps regulate an individual's relationship with the Creator, themselves, and everything in the environment. Islam identifies that since human beings are a creation, it must view that in the correct context and understand that there are needs and affairs of the people that require solutions. These needs and affairs are recognized and correctly organized so the people can have their affairs resolved in a right manner, including material progress through scientific and technological advancement. When Islam was implemented, all of society took the benefits of the advancements of the time. Unlike today, we have progressed materialistically, but not all of society is reaping the benefits. Basic needs such as clean water and electricity, are still a dire need and problem for many people in the world, and unfortunately, have not been resolved comprehensively by any charity work or organization.

Mindset Affects How We Learn

The interesting thing about learning science is the mindset and perspective from which it is taught and learned. We can see that in today's educational system, science and religion are taught as separate entities. And it is expected that anyone who views science from that perspective is doing science correctly. However, those who say that they can be integrated are vilified because science is a discipline that explains phenomena that are measurable, testable, and observable. Since God and religion are not tangible items that can be analyzed and explained with data, therefore, they are not compatible with science.

But the Muslim civilization never viewed science from that aspect. According to Ibn Sina:

"True science is science that seeks knowledge of the essence of things in relation to their divine origin."

Studying science meant that we would be able to understand certain phenomena in the context of how they exist. We would use those laws to understand nature and use that to appreciate the existence of Allah ﷻ because nature is a work of Allah ﷻ, (Iqbal, 1999). The Quran compels humans to ponder on the skies and stars, and the alteration of night and day. A 16th-century Persian Sufi poet and scholar, 'Abd al-Rahman Jami (d 1492) prayed to God:

O God; deliver us from the preoccupation with worldly vanities, and "show us the nature of things as they really are." Remove from our eyes the veil of ignorance and show us things as they really are. Show us not non-existence as existent, nor cast the veil of non-existence over the beauty of existence. Make this phenomenal world the mirror to reflect the manifestation of Thy beauty, not a veil to separate and repel us from Thee. Cause these unreal phenomena of the Universe to be for us the source of knowledge and insight, not the causes of ignorance and blindness. Our alienation and severance from Thy beauty all proceed from ourselves. Deliver us from ourselves, and accord to us intimate knowledge of Thee.

It is also part of the Islamic belief that there are things we do not know and have not discovered. This is Al-Ghayb, the unseen and unknown. Allah ﷻ says:

وَعِندَهُۥ مَفَاتِحُ ٱلْغَيْبِ لَا يَعْلَمُهَآ إِلَّا هُوَ ۚ وَيَعْلَمُ مَا فِى ٱلْبَرِّ وَٱلْبَحْرِ ۚ وَمَا تَسْقُطُ مِن وَرَقَةٍ إِلَّا يَعْلَمُهَا وَلَا حَبَّةٍ فِى ظُلُمَٰتِ ٱلْأَرْضِ وَلَا رَطْبٍ وَلَا يَابِسٍ إِلَّا فِى كِتَٰبٍ مُّبِينٍ

With Him are the keys of the unseen (ghayb). No one knows them other than Him. He knows what is in land and sea. No leaf falls but He knows it; nor there is a grain in the darkness of the earth or a green or dry thing but in a manifest Book. (6:59) [32]

Muslim psychologists of the time defined Al-Ghayb as the things that are beyond one's consciousness. Islamic belief states that human beings are limited, therefore the mind is also limited. Due to this limitation, the mind can't comprehend what is beyond its capacity. Muslim scientists described searching for answers about the metaphysical or unseen world, as dangerous because the mind was not designed nor prepared to sense metaphysical properties. They viewed this as a cause of mental and physical diseases. Humans are a physical object that are part of a physical world, and they can only comprehend what is visible and felt to them. So, humans should be satisfied with the metaphysical through religious revelation, spirituality, and philosophical discussion, and use their knowledge and enthusiasm to contribute to the improvement of the physical world that they inhabit.

When science and religion become separated, a gap in the understanding of the physical and metaphysical world exists, as one can't explain one without the other. Allah ﷻ is among the things that we can't see, yet we believe in Him ﷻ. That is because where there is Al-Ghayb, we have *Iman* (faith). Imagine trying to "see" pain as a wavelength or number scale. Could we really see pain as a physical object that we can measure in units and claim that this person's pain was either 2 centimeters or 2 meters long? We describe pain by what we feel, and we believe in it. Yet, what if we tried to smell a color? Are we really smelling a color in its originality or because we have associated that color with something in our physical world? Allah ﷻ says:

وَمَا لَهُم بِهِۦ مِنْ عِلْمٍ إِن يَتَّبِعُونَ إِلَّا ٱلظَّنَّ وَإِنَّ ٱلظَّنَّ لَا يُغْنِى مِنَ ٱلْحَقِّ شَيْئًا

"And they have no knowledge thereof. They follow but a guess, and a guess can never take the place of the truth." (53:28) [32]

"A little science distances you from God, but a lot of science brings you nearer to Him."— Louis Pasteur

Muslim Achievements Under Islam

Muslim students must understand that under Islamic rule, many great scientists and thinkers were produced. When Islamic civilization ruled from Spain all the way to Indonesia, Muslims felt a great responsibility of handling the affairs of all its citizens. In the ayah below, Allah ﷻ gave the Muslims an important task of leadership and spreading good among the society. These verses show the inspiration Muslims had that led to the Islamic Golden Age of Science and Technology.

Allah ﷻ has given Muslims a special status. He ﷻ said:

كُنْتُمْ خَيْرَ أُمَّةٍ أُخْرِجَتْ لِلنَّاسِ تَأْمُرُوْنَ بِالْمَعْرُوْفِ وَتَنْهَوْنَ عَنِ الْمُنْكَرِ وَتُؤْمِنُوْنَ بِاللهِ

"You are now the best people brought forth for (the guidance and reform of) mankind. You enjoin what is right and forbid what is wrong and believe in Allah." (3:110) [32]

Unfortunately, Muslim communities today are struggling to preserve their culture and heritage. Our children go to schools that are primarily taught history from the viewpoint of white supremacy. World history textbooks focus on Roman and Greek empires and suddenly jump to the European renaissance and industrial revolution. Nowhere in the textbooks does it mention about other civilizations and their contribution to the world. There is a gap of a 1000 years of non-European civilizations. This has caused Muslims to be deprived of their own history and is largely a result of the current educational system that is followed by many Muslim and non-Muslim countries. Rather, success and advancement were associated with Western and Eurocentrism while Muslim lands were associated with backwardness and in need of reformation.

Over the last few decades, immense work and research has been focused on reviving the Muslim civilization and achievements so that current and future generations can benefit from the knowledge and history that has shaped the modern world as we see today. Without the Muslim contributions between the 8th and 18th centuries, Europe wouldn't have seen its Renaissance period at all.

Some of the well-known accomplishments of Muslim scientists and thinkers include:

- Ibn Sina (Avicenna) – famous physician from Bukhara
- Ibn Nafis – physician who described cardiovascular circulation
- Al-Haytham – physicist, explained how light travels in the eye
- Ibn Khaldun – a philosopher and thinker
- Ibn Battuta – traveled across the globe
- Al-Khwarizmi – mathematician and father of algebra

In the field of medicine, Prophet Muhammad ﷺ insisted to people *"take medicines for your diseases,"* as people at that time were reluctant to do so.

Abu Huraira رضي الله عنه narrated that He ﷺ also said: *"Allah created no illness, but established for it a cure, except for old age. When the antidote is applied, the patient will recover with the permission of Allah." (Sahih al-Bukhari 5678)*[33]

Harun al Rashid was the famous Caliph in Baghdad of the Abbasid Empire that established the House of Wisdom (Dar ul Hikmah), and invited scholars of all backgrounds to come learn and collaborate on scientific topics. He established an observatory to promote the study of astronomy and had books translated from the previous Greek and Roman scientific knowledge. Al Rashid also established the first hospital in Baghdad. "It is highly probable that but for the Arabs, modern European civilization would never have arisen at all; it is absolutely certain that but for them, it would not have assumed that character which has enabled it to transcend all previous phases of evolution. (Briffault, 1938)

The list goes on in terms of the successes and accomplishments of the Muslims. Anyone who is keen to understand the truth can see that Islam never hindered the successful advancement of science and technology for material progress. There is a drastic difference between the situation of the European civilizations with the Muslim civilizations due to the implementation of Islam. It was because Islam never ignored that human beings are a special creation, and they will have to handle their affairs while in the dunya (world), and for that, advancement and material progress was very important to extract solutions for a society that would continue to exist. Science will become stagnant under systems and beliefs that do not prioritize the need to handle the affairs of human beings and to come up with creative and comprehensive solutions. Conclusively, Islam always welcomed and gave importance to attaining knowledge.

"Great indeed is the crime against religion committed by anyone who supposes that Islam is to be championed by the denial of mathematical sciences. For the revealed Law nowhere undertakes to deny or affirm these sciences, and the latter nowhere address themselves to religious matters."— Imam al-Ghazali (1058-1111)

Science Activities

This section contains a list of science topics and investigation prompts for educators, parents and kids to complete together or individually.

1. In the Qu'ran, Allah ﷻ dedicated a chapter to the spider, Surah Ankabut. He ﷻ describes those who have associated partners with Him as people who have taken the wrong path and have sought in a weak shelter. *"The likeness of those who have taken other patrons than Allah, is the likeness of a spider, which makes itself a dwelling; and the weakest of all dwellings is the dwelling of a spider." (29:41)* [32]

   a. Middle-High School (6th – 12th): Investigate why associating allies or partners with Allah ﷻ is like building a weak web? (Inquiry Based)

   b. Elementary School (K – 5th): Find out what is a spider's web made of and why is it a weak home? (Discovery learning)

   c. Elementary/Middle School (K – 8th): Construct a spider's web using different polygon shapes. (Hands-on/Activity Based, Math Integration)

2. The honey Bee is mentioned in Surah An-Nahl. Allah ﷻ describes the important jobs of the honey bees. He ﷻ also mentions the properties of honey and how honey is used. *"And your Lord inspired the bee, Take for yourself among the mountains, houses [i.e., hives], and among the trees and [in] that which they construct. Then eat from all the fruits and follow the ways of your Lord laid down [for you]. There emerges from their bellies a drink, varying in colors, in which there is healing for people. Indeed, that is a sign for people who give thought."*

   (16: 68-69) [32]

   a. Middle-High School (6th – 12th): Calculate the surface area of a hexagon compared to the surface area of a triangle or circle. How does this affect the ability of a honey bee to maximize its resources and energy? (Inquiry Based, Math Integration)

b. Elementary School (K - 5th): Construct a large hexagon out of cardboard or other recyclable materials. Then make smaller circles to fill the larger hexagon. Lastly, alter the circles by changing them into hexagons. Record and explain your observations about what you did and what happened during the process. Use the scientific method and write your responses. (Hands-on/Activity Based)

c. Middle School (5th – 8th): Research "The Honeybee Conjecture." Design a poster (physical/digital) explaining its meaning and what is the importance of the conjecture to honey bee life. (Research Prompt)

3. Of other surahs dedicated to specific animals, the ant also has one surah. The chapter itself describes the story of Suleyman عليه السلام 's army. One of the ants told their colony to quickly save themselves as Suleyman's army was close by. Allah ﷻ gave Suleyman عليه السلام special gifts like communicating with the animals so he heard what the ant said. It also showed that Suleyman عليه السلام was a humble and merciful prophet. Allah ﷻ describes all living things as: *"No creature is there crawling on the earth, no bird flying with its wings, but they are nations like unto yourselves. We have neglected nothing in the Book; then to their Lord they shall be mustered." (6:38)* [32]

a. Middle-High School (6th – 12th): Why is community so important to all living things? What does Islam say about community? Cite ayat from Qur'an that discusses how Muslims should take care of each other and stay connected as a community. (Inquiry Based)

b. Elementary School (K - 5th):

i. Build a food web, showing how ants consume their food and how they may be hunted by predators. (Research)

ii. Also try building your own ant farm. Experiment with the ants by building tunnels, offer them various foods, and track their behaviors. Write your observations in a notebook or make a video diary. (Discovery)

c. Middle School (5th – 8th): Most ants that we see are females. Investigate why females are important in ant colonies. How do ants transport seeds?

Research the process of how ants collect food and transport the food to their colonies. (Investigation/Research)

4. The eardrum is a special, thin membrane in the outer ear that helps you to hear. When sound waves hit the eardrum, the vibrations go to the inner ear through nerves to the part of the brain that helps us to hear. Allah ﷻ talks about how hearing and listening determine true believers from the hypocrites. *"And among them are those who listen to you, but We have placed over their heart coverings, lest they understand it, and in their ears deafness. And if they should see every sign, they will not believe in it. Even when they come to you arguing with you, those who disbelieve say, 'This is not but legends of the former peoples.'" (6:25)* [32]

a. Middle-High School (6th – 12th):

i. How do we actually hear sound? Create a flowchart of the nerve pathways that help you to hear. Start with the sound entering the outer ear to the brain. Define each part of the process. Use pictures to show what is happening in each part of the hearing pathway. (Inquiry Based)

ii. Who were the Muslim scientists that made contributions to medical science in regards to the ear structure and anatomy? Research what they did and what was the common medical belief at the time.

b. Elementary School (K – 5th): Describe the sensory organs and each sense every living thing has. Make a table of each sense, using pictures, and list what each sense does and why they are so important. (Discovery)

c. Middle School (5th – 8th): Investigate how cochlear implants are placed. Why do patients have to get a cochlear implant and how does it improve the lives of those who receive one? (Investigation)

5. Allah ﷻ is the creator of all things. By His ﷻ will, all living things were created with special attributes and features. Humans have special traits on the tips of their fingers called fingerprints. These are different for every human being. Fingerprints are used to help identify an individual for security and criminal purposes. Allah ﷻ says: *"Does man think that We will not assemble his bones? Yes. [We are] Able [even] to proportion his fingertips." (75:3-4)* [32]

a. Middle-High School (5th – 12th): Forensic Science is a field of biology that uses different testing and investigation methods to solve criminal and legal issues. You can apply the same testing methods as forensic scientists do in your own home. In a group or individually, touch various surfaces and label each one with a number or letter. After 2 days and then again after 5 days, go back to the surfaces you touched. Dust the surfaces using baby powder (or another kind of talcum powder) or cocoa powder for lighter surfaces. Use a paint brush or blush makeup brush to sweep away the excess. Then take transparent tape (large packing tape) and gently place the tape over the surface and pick up the fingerprint and place it on a white background paper or cardstock. Now have each of your household members, friends, or whoever you choose to do this project with, make their own fingerprints using an ink pad. Compare the results with the results from the surfaces and see who touches what surface just by using fingerprints. Record your observations and explain how fingerprints and forensic technology have contributed to criminal investigations. (Investigation)

b. Elementary School (K – 5th): Using different color ink pads, make fingerprints of each of your fingers on both hands on a poster or sketch paper. Observe the different shapes of each of your fingerprints. Decide which color ink gave the best fingerprint result. Record your observations in a notebook or video diary. Compare your results with your siblings or friends. (Discovery)

Other Topics:

Take a look at the list below to discover and learn about other topics that the Qu'ran discusses or find something in the Qu'ran that makes you curious. Is there something you want to know and learn more about? Will you make the next scientific discovery?

- Soil
- Embryology
- Justice and Law
- Inheritance
- Women's Rights

- Genetics
- Water
- Solar system: planets, orbits, universe
- Natural Disasters: earthquakes and floods
- Mountains
- Animals
- Fruits and Vegetables
- Creation and the Beginning of Time

References

1. Holstermann, Nina & Grube, Dietmar & Bögeholz, Susanne. (2010). Hands-on Activities and Their Influence on Students' Interest. Research in Science Education. 40. 743-757. 10.1007/s11165-009-9142-0.
2. Kaushik, Vibha. (2020). The Study of the effectiveness of the inquiry-based learning method in chemistry teaching learning process.
3. Savion, L. (2009). Clinging to discredited beliefs: The larger cognitive story. *Journal of the Scholarship of Teaching and Learning, 9,* 81-92.
4. Madhyastha & Tanimoto (2009). Faring with facets: Building and using databases of student misconceptions. http://jime.open.ac.uk/2009/01/jime-2009-01.html
5. Aziz, N., 2018. *The Mystery of Fingerprint in Al Quran.* [online] Iosrjournals.org. Available at: <http://www.iosrjournals.org/iosr-jhss/papers/Vol.%2023%20Issue2/Version-3/D2302032330.pdf> [Accessed 27 May 2021].
6. Goldsmith, P. A. (2006). Learning to understand inequality and diversity: Getting students past ideologies. *Teaching Sociology, 34*(3), 263-277.
7. Northern Illinois University Center for Innovative Teaching and Learning. (2020). Howard Gardner's theory of multiple intelligences. In *Instructional guide for university faculty and teaching assistants.* Retrieved from https://www.niu.edu/citl/resources/guides/instructional-guide
8. Gardner, H. (2013). Frequently asked questions—Multiple intelligences and related educational topics. Retrieved from https://howardgardner01.files.wordpress.com/2012/06/faq_march2013.pdf

9. Arlusi, N., & Fuad, A. (2020). Relasi Nilai Mata Kuliah Tasawuf dengan Akhlak Mahasiswa Institut Agama Islam Tribakti (IAIT) Kediri. *Indonesian Journal Of Islamic Education Studies (IJIES)*, *3*(1), 96-111. https://doi.org/10.33367/ijies.v3i1.1250
10. Raashed, D., & Raashed, D. (2019). *The Qur'an appeals to human intelligence*. AMUST. Retrieved 10 June 2021, from https://www.amust.com.au/2019/07/the-quran-appeals-to-human-intelligence/.
11. *Scientific Approach of the Quran | CPS International*. Cpsglobal.org. (2021). Retrieved 10 June 2021, from https://www.cpsglobal.org/content/scientific-approach-quran.
12. Suhag, A., Lashari, A., Malik, D., & Memon, F. (2019). Impact of Science Teaching Methodologies on Students' Performance, in Sindh Province of Pakistan: A Case Study of Secondary Schools in Khairpur Mir's District. *US-China Foreign Language*, *17*(12). https://doi.org/10.17265/1539-8080/2019.12.004
13. Hassan, S., & Ibrahim, A. (2021). *The Art of Teaching Science in Secondary Schools: A Meta Analysis*. Files.eric.ed.gov. Retrieved 10 June 2021, from https://files.eric.ed.gov/fulltext/EJ1165738.pdf.
14. Iqbal, M. (1999). *What Makes Islamic Science Islamic? | National Center for Science Education*. Ncse.ngo. Retrieved 10 June 2021, from https://ncse.ngo/what-makes-islamic-science-islamic.
15. Sparks, S. (2019). *Students Learn More From Inquiry-Based Teaching, International Study Finds*. Education Week. Retrieved 10 June 2021, from https://www.edweek.org/teaching-learning/students-learn-more-from-inquiry-based-teaching-international-study-finds/2019/10.
16. Kola, J., & Langenhoven, K. (2015). *TEACHING METHOD IN SCIENCE EDUCATION: THE NEED FOR A PARADIGM SHIFT TO PEER INSTRUCTION (PI) IN NIGERIAN SCHOOLS*. Idpublications.org. Retrieved 10 June 2021, from https://www.idpublications.org/wp-content/uploads/2015/07/TEACHING-METHOD-IN-SCIENCE-EDUCATION-THE-NEED-FOR-A-PARADIGM-SHIFT-TO-PEER-INSTRUCTION.pdf.
17. Walsh, C. (2008). *Where science and religion meet, from an Islamic perspective*. Harvard Gazette. Retrieved 10 June 2021, from https://news.harvard.edu/gazette/story/2008/05/where-science-and-religion-meet-from-an-islamic-perspective/.
18. Afridi, M. (2013). *Contribution of Muslim Scientists to the World: An Overview of Some Selected Fields*. Core.ac.uk. Retrieved 10 June 2021, from https://core.ac.uk/download/pdf/300424246.pdf.
19. Wani, Z., & Maqbool, T. (2012). *The Islamic Era and Its Importance to Knowledge and the Development of Libraries*. DigitalCommons@University

of Nebraska - Lincoln. Retrieved 10 June 2021, from https://digitalcommons.unl.edu/libphilprac/718/.
20. Hill, M. (2011). *The Critical Thinking Muslim*. Margari Aziza. Retrieved 10 June 2021, from https://margariaziza.com/2011/08/27/the-critical-thinking-muslim/.
21. Al-Hassani, S. (2012). *A 1000 Years Amnesia: Sports in Muslim Heritage - Muslim Heritage*. Muslim Heritage. Retrieved 10 June 2021, from https://muslimheritage.com/a-1000-years-amnesia-sports-in-muslim-heritage/.
22. Mineo, L. (2020). *Harvard historian examines how textbooks taught white supremacy*. Harvard Gazette. Retrieved 10 June 2021, from https://news.harvard.edu/gazette/story/2020/09/harvard-historian-examines-how-textbooks-taught-white-supremacy/.
23. Yacovone, D. (2018). *Teaching White Supremacy: U.S. History Textbooks and the Influence of Historians*. Medium. Retrieved 10 June 2021, from https://medium.com/houstonmarshall/teaching-white-supremacy-u-s-history-textbooks-and-the-influence-of-historians-b614c5d2781b.
24. Briffault, Robert. "The Making of Humanity" London, 1938.
25. Al Khateeb, Firas, "Lost Islamic History" Hurst Publications, 2014
26. Al Khilafah Publications, London, 2002
27. Ashy, M., 2021. *Health and Illness from an Islamic Perspective*. [online] Patch Adams Organization. Available at: <http://www.jstor.org/stable/27511376?origin=JSTOR-pdf> [Accessed 10 June 2021].
28. Al-Gesir, N. (1961). The Story of Faith in Philosophy, Science and The Quran. Beirut: The Islamic Office
29. Galindo, J., n.d. *Revealing & Dealing with Misconceptions*. [online] Ablconnect.harvard.edu. Available at: <https://ablconnect.harvard.edu/revealing-and-dealing-misconceptions> [Accessed 10 June 2021].
30. Inventionland Institute. n.d. *Discovery Learning Method - Inventionland Institute*. [online] Available at: <https://inventionlandinstitute.com/discovery-learning-method> [Accessed 10 June 2021].
31. Chalmers, M. (2003). The Scavenger Hunt As an Interactive Teaching Tool to Develop Research Skills. Interface: The Journal of Education, Community and Values 3(6). Available http://bcis.pacificu.edu/journal/2003/06/chalmers.php
32. The Holy Quran – Quran Verses. Translation by Sahih International
33. Hadith – Sahih Al-Bukhari

CHAPTER 4

The Teaching and Learning of History

Mariam Seddiq

My students often question why they are studying history. They find the past irrelevant to their lives and don't want to become historians. This may come across as a simplistic teenage vent expressing their disinterest and disconnect with history but there is a deeper sentiment here. Allah ﷻ has created us with a purpose and it's in our fitrah (nature) to find a purpose in all that we do.

"We only created the heavens and the earth and everything in between for a purpose and an appointed term. Yet the disbelievers are turning away from what they have been warned about." (Qur'an, Surat Al-'Ahqaf 46:3)

Islam gives the subject of history a clear purpose and direction, which is to seek morals, understanding and wisdom. In the works of early Muslim historians, we see how historical investigation was pursued to not merely demonstrate our critical thinking and analytical skills but to find the truth and gain moral lessons.

Qur'anic view of history

Islam as a comprehensive religion gives us the wisdom and explanation as to why we study and teach history. Two-thirds of the Qur'an refers to historical events and nations. It is in the story of Prophet Nuh (peace be upon him) that we appreciate the patience of one man's 950 years quest to convey the message of the oneness of God. We learn what befell his people who rejected his message, and a similar fate befell other societies such as the people of Hud and Madyan and Thamud. While in the story of Musa and Harun (peace be upon them) facing the Pharaoh, the lesson of faith, perseverance, and the consequences of our actions is reiterated. This narrative continues in the stories of Qarun, people of the cave, Namrud, Prophet Ibraheem (peace be upon him) and so forth. Allah ﷻ reminds us that:

"Have they not travelled throughout the land to see what was the end of those before them? Allah annihilated them, and a similar fate awaits the disbelievers." (Qur'an, Surah Muhammad 47:10)

In the Qur'an, Allah ﷻ directly explains that the purpose of narrating the stories of past nations and societies is to learn lessons from.

"In their stories there is truly a lesson for people of reason. This message cannot be a fabrication, rather it is a confirmation of previous revelation, a detailed explanation of all things, a guide, and a mercy for people of faith." (Qur'an, Surah Yusuf 12:111)

History serves a profound purpose in Islam. Its lessons are an incentive for the believers to follow in the footsteps of the righteous. It is a source of education for the ummah as it proves the prophethood of Muhammad (peace be upon him) and distinguishes his followers. In the hadith of 'ifk (slander against the mother-of-the-believers, Aisha, may Allah ﷻ be please with her), we learn that it was through the patience of Prophet Yusuf (peace be upon him) that Aisha رضي الله عنها found solace and comfort. Allah ﷻ thus reminds the believers:

"We shall tell you all the stories of the messengers (of old) through which we shall steady your heart. You will find in them the truth and an exhortation and something to be remembered for the believers." (Qur'an, Surah Hud 11:120)

It is in history that we witness people's legacy. A famous Arab saying reminds us that "A tale is all a person leaves behind. Strive that your tale be known as good and kind." Clearly Muslims understood the countless merits of studying history. The Muslim historian, 'Ali al-Mas'udi (d.956), wrote: "History is a branch of knowledge enjoyed by both scholars and ignorant persons and relished by both the stupid and the intelligent. Everything remarkable becomes known through history. Every marvel achieves appreciation through it…History collects for you… insufficiency and abundance…many judgements are based upon history. The knowledge of it is an asset in any gathering and station." In the Muslim world, history became an intellectual endeavour and as the medium to increase one's knowledge and wisdom. While the layman has always seen history as a source of entertainment, it is the educated who appreciate it as an opportunity to learn, grow, and 'nourish his soul and imagination'.

Knowledge of history has always been popular in the Muslim world. To be an educated individual, one was required to have knowledge of history, whether to work in politics as a vizier or a government secretary. Muslims were eager to study past empires, this included the Greeks, Persians, Romans and most importantly the early Islamic history such as the Khulafah ar-Rashidun. Even Muslim soldiers were keen to learn about the early Islamic conquests and the biographies of distinguished Muslims. The Ottoman empire was particularly known for reviewing their previous battles and taking notes in their preparation for their upcoming expeditions. Attention was also given to preserving historical sources. This included letters of the Prophet to leaders inviting them to Islam, government papers, official declaration or speeches, and even international treaties. History thus became an essential source of information because writing and recording about the society and its people, geography, typography was essentially to not only acknowledge the very existence of these societies, but it enabled the historian and the public to better understand societies and its governments. Next to the Qur'an and Sunnah, history and biography became an important subject to study. It enabled the believers to compare different civilisations, their politics, and societies to gain wisdom and seek guidance for a better society and avoid past shortcomings. The study of history was clearly seen as a sign for the believers to avoid disobeying Allah ﷻ. In numerous verses, Allah ﷻ states:

"And an exhortation for those who fear God." (Qur'an, Surah Al-Baqarah 2:62)

The English word *history* is derived from Greek, *historia*, meaning 'finding out' or 'narrative' or a 'learned or wise' man. The general understanding is that history is a civilisation's accounts of its past. During the 9th century the Muslims first began to use two Arabic words for history: *tarikh* and *'ilm al-ahbar'*. The word *tarikh* means a specific time or era while '*ilm al-ahbar*' is translated in English as 'historiography', the science of history. Ibn Khaldun, the famous Muslim historiographer of the 14th century, defined history as events that are peculiar to an age or race. The Muslims regarded history as the stories or anecdotes about 'remarkable events', the consequences of human actions, and the dates associated with those events.

Tarikh or time is an important aspect of history as it gives structure and clarity to events and chronicles. The importance of time is well established in the Qur'an; however, its focus is didactic. In Surah al-Asr (*the time*), Allah ﷻ reflects on how man is in loss and destruction because of how he uses his time; except for those who believe in Allah, do righteous deeds, enjoin the truth and patience then they are those who are saved. Islam emphasises the need to focus on what is essential and the focus on tarikh should be on what is indispensable to people and events. This is obvious in numerous stories in the Qur'an where detail was there to gain a moral message. The number of the people of the cave in Surah Kahf is an interesting example. Allah ﷻ reminds us that people were in doubt as to how many they were in the cave, and they kept questioning and wondering. But what is important, their number or why they were there? It is this didactic perspective that should resonate through our historical inquiry. As Ibn Khaldun pointed out, we should seek the bigger questions - why and how events took place should be a central focus of our history lessons.

The First Muslim Historians

In the modern era, historical accounts have been widely regarded as biased narratives with the sole goal of glorifying leaders and empires. However, Islam some 1400 years ago changed this culture by making the pursuit of truth a fundamental aspect of historical inquiry. This practice began during the time of the Prophet which influenced the collection of hadith literature. The Prophet had admonished his companions regarding honesty and narrating true accounts. In the Sahih Muslim (Book 45, Hadith 136), 'Abdullah reported Allah's Messenger ﷺ as saying: "It is obligatory for you to tell the truth, for truth leads to virtue and virtue leads to Paradise, and the man who continues to speak the truth and endeavours to tell the truth is eventually recorded as truthful with Allah ﷻ, and beware of telling of a lie for telling of a lie leads to obscenity and obscenity leads to Hell-Fire, and the person who keeps telling lies and endeavours to tell a lie is recorded as a liar with Allah ﷻ." In another hadith collected in Jami` at-Tirmidhi (Vol. 4, Book 11, Hadith 2518), Al-Hasan bin 'Ali said: "I remember that the Messenger of Allah ﷺ said: 'Leave what makes you in doubt for what does not make you in doubt. The truth brings tranquillity while falsehood sows doubt." The Prophet had directly warned the believers of conjecture and its seriousness as a grave lie. It was a religious duty to be truthful and honest in conveying information, avoiding unfounded conjecture or slander, and in this pursuit of 'truth' the liars were to be exposed. The Qur'an also emphasises that:

"If a wicked man brings you some news, strive to get clarification." (Qur'an, Surah *al-Hujurāt* 49:6)

The first Muslim historians were the scholars of hadith who demonstrated how to approach historical inquiry. They assessed and evaluated the hadith transmitters (known as isnad) and their biographies. This scrutiny involved examining the merits and demerits of the narrators of hadith to verify whether their accounts were truthful and reliable. The hadith transmitters were judged according to their moral character, having a continuous link to the Prophet ﷺ, being proficient in both memory and writing, their transmitted hadith was compared to a stronger authority and did not contradict the stronger authority, and that their hadith was compared to other hadith to verify that no hidden defects existed. All five categories had to be met for a hadith to be graded sahih (authentic). If it failed the moral character requirement then the hadith was totally rejected, but if it failed in any other category it was labelled as hasan (agreeable). This meticulous science ensured that only reliable narrations were accepted. It became known as the science of hadith or '*Ilm al-Jarh wa Ta'dil* (literally translated as the science of criticism or praise). This science was established in the first century of Islam and was regarded as the foundation of Islam through which the Qur'an is explained, and Islamic law is clarified. It is for this reason that meticulous care was given to it. Imam Bukhari (d.870), a famous hadith scholar, spent twenty years collecting the ahadith into his book, *Sahih Bukhari* in which he only included sahih hadith.

During the second century of Hijrah, Muslims laid the foundation of historiography – the science of recording history through critical study of sources using reason and intellectual assessment. This was pioneered by scholars such as Ibn Sa'd (d.845), al-Tabari (d.923), al-Mas'udi (d.956), and later scholars such as Ibn Athir (d.1233), and Ibn Kathir (d.1373). Their emphasis was on thoroughly studying the historical sources which was essentially following the science of hadith. However, there is a difference between historiography and science of hadith, as it is difficult to apply the five categories of hadith authentication in general history. Nevertheless, the general aim of establishing what was reliable from unreliable and differentiating between truth and falsehood was the perspective that underpinned the science of hadith and set the foundation for historiography. Muslim historians questioned the accuracy of the information and how the events were recorded and reported. They were expected to avoid slander and gossip and adhere to the values that Islam calls, which include fairness, exactness, truth, and fear of God. And not to be influenced by personal bias. These historians were aware that sources are created and influenced by personal motivation and could be false. They thus judged historians for their motivation and purpose and carefully sifted their work to identify contradiction and incoherence.

The focus of Muslim historians was to identify what was historically essential and aimed to present events coherently. They were motivated with useful knowledge, to gain wisdom and attain the success of this world and hereafter. Their focus was always to gain didactic or instructive stories. The famous historical text included Ibn Kathir's *Bidayah wa Nihayah*, and al-Kutubi's (d.1363) *Uyun al-Tawarik*. Muslim historians such as al-Tabari, whose work is seen as a model example for later historians, demonstrated how his philosophical and inquiry approach was very much influenced by his Islamic worldview. As a jurist and well-versed in politics, he gave particular attention on recording the seerah (biography of the Prophet ﷺ) with an annalistic focus. He was meticulous in examining the sources and the chain of transmitters, sometimes he placed different accounts side by side to emphasise the different reports, or he even included foreign words or specific quotations to ensure that his work remained accurate.

By the 14th century, the principles of historiography were well established by the Muslim historian and philosopher Abd-ar-Rahman Abu Zayd Ibn Muhammad Ibn Khaldun al-Hadrami (1332-1406). Ibn Khaldun wrote an eight-volume series exploring the nature of society and theories of why things happen. The first volume has been translated as *al-Muqaddimah*, in which he examined why empires fall and rise to power. He studied the different economic, social, political and religious factors that cause events to take place. Ibn Khaldun was the first Muslim and world historian to apply theory in understanding history. He argued that history is not regurgitating facts but rather it is about making conclusions. His book presents a thorough explanation of historiography making it the first detailed text on this subject. The famed British historian, Arnold I. Toynbee regarded his book as "undoubtably the greatest work of its kind that has ever yet been created by any mind in any time or place."

Ibn Khaldun reiterated that Islam is a civilisation with its own principles and values that should define and mandate how we approach history. The purpose of history he argued is to 'establish the truth', which is the principle of the Qur'an – to seek the truth and avoid falsehood. He stressed that it is the duty of historians to seek the 'truth' in history and see it as a guide to gain beneficial lessons (ibrar). To achieve this, Ibn Khaldun emphasised that historians must apply a critical eye and should not be seduced by merely entertaining the masses or parroting one another. He argued that historical sources project the narrator's view of the world, which is fundamentally shaped by power, identity, and tradition. It is thus imperative that historical narratives are assessed to identify who the narrator is and what has influenced their account. In essence this approach follows the sciences of hadith in seeking the truth. Ibn Khaldun held a pragmatic perspective and focused on the reality of the source; to identify bias in the source, historians are required to be thorough in their research of sources, be knowledgeable in the subject, whether it is the people, their customs, traditions, politics, and societies. To address the validity of historical accounts, Ibn Khaldun emphasised that historians should be well grounded in the knowledge of the event but also make judgments and assess the accounts for errors and misleading information. History is undoubtedly a construct, and these sources need to be assessed and carefully scrutinised.

Ibn Khaldun's work and the principles of historiography was very much reflected in the works of Muslim historians and society. The Ottoman empire particularly took interest in Ibn Khaldun's theory of the lifespan of empires. Which he described to be equivalent to a human lifespan of approximately 100-120 years. During these 100 years, three generations would rule. The first generation would generally be from a rough background without much luxury and would conquer cities and establish itself. The later generations would be weakened by their luxury and would be overthrown. The Ottomans, however, outlasted this lifespan and ruled for 600 years but the trajectory of their rise and fall reflected Ibn Khaldun's theory. In the Ottoman historical writings, we sense how the preservation of the empire, and its power was given priority and there was little blind devotion to the leader. The biography of Sultan Fatih Mehmed, *Tarih-I Abu'l-Fath,* History of the Conqueror, the 7th sultan of the Ottoman empire, written by Tursun Beg (b.1426-d. unknown), is an example of this. It is considered widely as the most historically accurate account of Mehmed's life as Tursun, who was an eyewitness to Mehmed's court, was meticulous in accessing government documents and avoided topics that he wasn't familiar with. After Mehmed II's death, Tursun presented this biography to Mehmed's son, Bayzid II, and Tursun wrote that Mehmed was promptly forgotten because attention was turned to the serious business of running the empire. In his introduction he clarified that the purpose of his work was to advise Bayzid II on how to rule effectively. He highlighted five moral virtues (wisdom, courage, honesty, and justice, and fear of God) that would ensure the success of the sultan and that of the empire and its people. In following with the Islamic values, history was thus presented as *nasiha*, advice and guidance to the rulers.

History in the non-Muslim world

In Europe the scientific approach to studying history emerged gradually, some 300 years after Ibn Khaldun's book. And prior to the 17th century there were no serious attempts by past civilisations to engage in historical inquiry. The ancient Egyptians, Chinese, Mesopotamians merely exalted their leaders and their exploits. Even the historical accounts in the Hebrew

Bible were never examined for reliability. There are chapters in the New Testament whose authors are unknown. While the earliest Greek philosophers, such as Hecataeous of Miletus (c.490 BCE) and Heradotus (the 'father of history) did note that 'silly fables' were rife, they never pursued a detailed study of authenticating sources. These Greek historians, such as Thucydides and later Roman historians continued writing annals (chronicles) without engaging in historical inquiry. It was only in the 16th century, and after learning much from the Muslim world, that the Europeans began to explore historiography. The very first booklet in Europe on historical method was written in the 16th century by Jean Bodin. In the 18th century Europeans scholars showed scepticism and questioned reliability of sources. However, it was in the 19th century in Germany that historiography was given an academic focus. It was led by Leopold von Ranke (d.1886) who stressed the importance of verifying facts and closely examining sources.

During the age of reason or modernity, which took root in the 18-19th century Europe, a materialistic approach to understanding history emerged in western academia. This worldly focus denied the divine message or role in the course of human history. A worldview that was very much in conflict with Christianity particularly with Catholicism as it bolstered the scientific inquiry and perspective, which was also fuelled by the industrial economic and political worldviews. These interpretations included either the philosophical viewpoint of G.W. Hegel (1770-1831), or the viewpoint of Karl Marx (1818-1883) which focused on man's materialistic motivation in his decision making and course of action. Marx ignored the human conscience and focused on the class system and economics. While Arnold Toynbee (1889-1975) argued that man is influenced by his environment and location, Islam, however, acknowledges man's free will in shaping his destiny. This narrative is explained in Surah al-Baqarah, which describes man's journey as the creation of God, blessed with the guidance to differentiate between good and evil and pursue the right course of action. God created the world with clear laws (sunnah) highlighting the rise and fall of civilisation, the trajectory of human history.

It is clear that understanding history is very much influenced by varied perspectives and interpretations. For instance, the Ottoman rise to power could be viewed from many angles such as economic, political or religious. A Marxist perspective would try to prove that the trade routes and the wealth was the motivating forces in the rise of the Ottoman state. However, as Muslims we can also see that religion played an important role. This is evident in the religious scholarship and the widespread presence of the madrasa in the Ottoman rule and expansion. The reason why in the west the religious factors is sidelined is that since the Enlightenment there is a push for a material understanding of the world and factors of influence, which focuses on the economic, social, or political dynamics of society rather than the religious values.

During the 20th century, the study of history became more controversial. This conflict centred on the notion of 'truth', called postmodernism. It focused on scientific rationality and reason to argue that historical knowledge is a construct and lacks objectivity making the past non-existent and relative. The focus of postmodernism is to critically analyse language, to be critical of values and claims of truth, emphasising that history is not progressive or impartial but that historians construct history. The postmodernists have questioned the status of history and argue that there is no ultimate truth. They argue that language is relative making meaning and the author's intent unstable. It is a contradictory dilemma because to assert that 'all language is 'unstable' makes the argument itself unstable. This great self-confidence with reason and science has sidelined belief. In addition, this obsession with rationality has brought science itself into question as not self-evident truth. The critic of postmodernism, Roger Scruton (d.2020), famously stated: "The man who tells you truth does not exist is asking you not to believe him. So don't."

History in the School System

Teachers play a crucial role in developing students' understanding and appreciation of history and historiography. This role is two-fold as it requires teachers to reflect on their methods as well as the needs of the students. A teacher's knowledge of the subject matter is ineffective when there is little or no understanding of the factors that influence learners and how they learn. While a teacher's knowledge of important facts as well as historical methods of inquiry provides the foundation for teaching history. It is also essential that teachers are aware and address how learners think and conceptualise about the past.

The teaching of history in western schools have been influenced by theories of cognitive development. The stages of cognitive development purposed by psychologist Jean Piaget (1896–1980) argues that children and most adolescents are unable to conceptualise time or abstract ideas. This means that at primary schools, history is taught through focus on personal and community history. It is also widely understood that students appreciate and understand history more when links are made to their backgrounds, beliefs, and experiences. In addition, a students' background influences how they approach history. Parents who appreciate history and its merits will nurture similar values in their children. In our capitalistic world, subjects such as science and mathematics are given more esteem as it generates money for the economy. Some parents may push their children to value such subjects as it will gain them university placement in high paying careers, and they may relegate history to an unimportant domain. This undoubtably will influence the students' attitude towards history and will undermine the benefits that they can gain from history.

One of the most valued aspects of history is to create critical thinkers who judge historical accounts and seek wisdom from our past. The historian and educator Martin Booth (d.2004) diverged from Piaget's theories and emphasised that adolescents have interpretive skills, which can be taught and nurtured through inquiry-based learning and developing an appreciation of empathy. The secondary schooling years have taken his approach in giving students the opportunity to analyse, interpret, reach historical hypothesis. This is not divergent from the Islamic approach in assessing sources and reaching the truth. In addition to developing historical skills, the purpose of history in schools has been to enrich students' moral values through appreciating the virtues of empathy, varied perspectives, and to engage in a discussion of moral choices. By addressing questions such as how and why events took place, students can reach moral conclusions and synthesise the evidence. In the western curriculum, history is viewed as an important avenue to teach civics and citizenship which involves democratic values and attitudes such as fostering social justice and rejecting racism. History in schools is thus viewed as an avenue to develop one's moral position and worldview.

Our beliefs and values have a significant influence on how we approach and teach history. This is evident in the research by Suzanne Wilson and Sam Wineburg who demonstrated the varied approaches taken by teachers based on their personal beliefs and values. They argued that teachers who see history as open to debate will encourage their students to question historical events. While teachers who see history as factual events will focus on embracing historical data. On the other hand, teachers who view history as the means to enshrine social change will focus on issues of gender, race, and power. Ronal Evans also delved into this research highlighting the varied types of history teachers as: storytellers who narrate and don't engage in a discussion; scientists who encourage questions, analysis, and debates to deconstruct the puzzle; relativists or reformers who approach history from a political or religious perspective and call for action; philosophers who focus on the consequences of past events; and liberals who focus on the intellectual role of history.

The focus that teachers give to teaching Islamic history is another important area of reflection. Islamic history has been slotted into medieval period suggesting that Islamic history ended in the 1500s. This view has been further complicated with a narrow study of ruling families, that of the Ummayads and Abbasids which ignores the civilisational contributions of the Muslim world and only focuses on the narrow ruling elites and their power struggles. The Muslim historian Imad al-Din Khalil specified five areas to focus on when studying Islamic history: 1) Political leadership; 2) Dawah and spread of Islam; 3) External challenges; 4) Society; 5) Islamic civilisation.

When we study history, it is necessary for us to understand and appreciate our worldview. Our beliefs, values, and life purpose shape how we view history and understand it. History is no longer a subject of chronicles but rather it is approached through a theoretical viewpoint, which endeavours to answer why and how things have happened. For the past two thousand years we have sufficient data to understand that events took place. These events have been studied from a different perspective, whether its economic, social or political. For Muslims, Islam plays a significant role in our lives whether it relates to politics, ethics, or morality or how we approach and interpret knowledge. While western historians view history as a 'constructed' interpretation of our world, from the Muslim perspective our aqeedah should define our approach to history. Our Qur'anic principles need to shape our approach to the writing and focus of history. The Qur'anic principles of finding the truth and abstaining from lies and conjecture is the platform of our historical inquiry. In addition, history is a reminder to the believers to remember, reflect and thus gain a beneficial lesson. The Islamic perspective sees history as a medium to not only understand humanity but also gain lessons. Muslims must see these moral lessons and wisdom as the path to the worship of Allah ﷻ because the sole purpose of creation is to worship Allah ﷻ.

Figure 1. Islam's guide on how to approach teaching and studying history

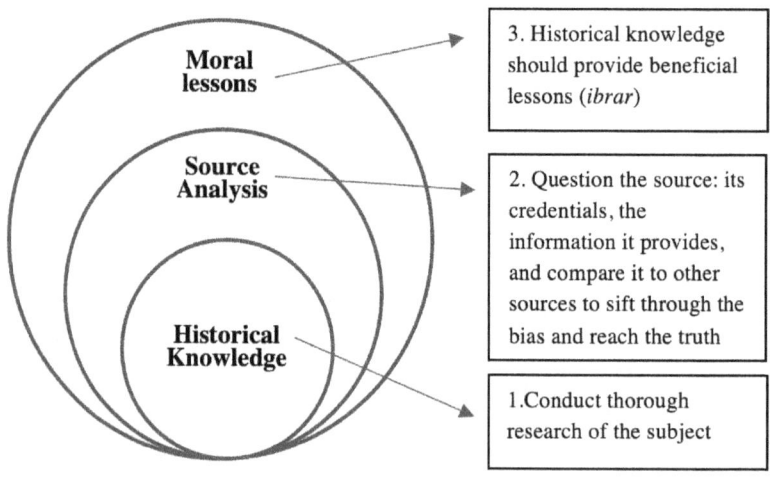

Integrating the Islamic perspective in the Australian National History Syllabus

When we approach the subject of history in the school system, it is necessary to reflect on our perspective and emphasis. A framework or set of principles should be considered to help support and address the needs of Muslim students. It involves:

1. Identifying the Islamic perspective – what is the Islamic position in relation to the historical events?
2. Identifying the strategies that will nurture the Islamic perspective and values
3. Identifying the Islamic moral lessons that can be derived from the historical subject

Sample Unit:

In teaching the Industrial Revolution to grade nine or ten students, we learn about all the factors that shaped this era and its long-term impacts. The central Islamic theme in this unit could focus on what motivates people's behaviour, drawing our attention to be mindful of our behaviour and its consequences.

Australian National History Syllabus Questions
- What were the changing features of the movement of peoples from 1750 to 1918?
- How did new ideas and technological developments contribute to change in this period?

Central questions that will identify and integrate the Islamic perspective in this unit:

⇒ What is Islam's position regarding migration?
⇒ How does Islam approach technological innovations and varying ideologies?
⇒ What Islamic lessons can be derived from the impact of the Industrial Revolution?

Mariam Seddiq | 60

Focus areas The technological innovations that led to the Industrial Revolution, and other conditions that influenced the industrialisation of Britain (the agricultural revolution, access to raw materials, wealthy middle class, cheap labour, transport system and expanding empire) and of Australia (ACDSEH017)	Activities/Strategies **nurturing the Islamic perspective:**
<ul><li>Outline the main reasons why the Industrial Revolution began in Britain</li><li>Describe the key features of the agricultural revolution in Britain, including the emergence of a cheap labour force, and describe the changes to the way of life of men and women who moved from the country to towns</li><li>Locate the growth and extent of the **British Empire from 1750–1900** and identify the raw materials Britain obtained from its empire, for example sugar from Jamaica, wool from Australia, and cotton and tea from India</li><li>Identify key inventors and their inventions and discuss how some of these inventions affected transport and manufacturing in this period</li><li>Explain how industrialisation contributed to the development of Britain and Australia in this period</li></ul>	⇒ Compare the British Empire to the Ottoman Empire – focusing on their motivation to expand and extend of their empire. ⇒ Students research the Islamic principles regarding migration and slavery.
The **population movements** and changing settlement patterns during this period (ACDSEH080)	
<ul><li>Outline and explain population movements in Britain, for example movement from country villages to towns and cities, and **emigration** to other countries</li></ul>	⇒ Students research about Islamic values regarding the rights of workers, children, and women.

The experiences of men, women and children during the Industrial Revolution, and their changing way of life (ACDSEH081) • Describe the changes to the way of life of men and women who moved from the country to towns and cities • Use a variety of sources to investigate **working conditions** in factories, mines and other occupations, with particular emphasis on **child labour** The **short and long-term impacts** of the Industrial Revolution, including global changes in landscapes, transport and communication (ACDSEH082) • Discuss **positive and negative consequences** of the Industrial Revolution, for example the growth of cities and pollution and the development of trade unions • Assess the short-term and long-term impacts of the Industrial Revolution, including global changes in landscapes, transport and communication	⇒ Students research about Muslim inventions: their purpose and impact of these inventions. Compare these inventions to the Industrial Revolution and explain what Islam says about the impact of our behaviour.

Reference:

Ahmed, Y. (2020, October 12). Muslims' Collective Amnesia of the Ottoman Past—and Why We Should Reclaim Our History. *The Young Ottomans*. Retrieved from https://www.theyoungottomans.com/muslims-collective-amnesia-of-the-ottoman-past-and-why-we-should-reclaim-our-history/

Ashraf, S.A. (1989). *The Qur'anic Concept of History*. Leicester: The Islamic Foundation.

Ibn, K., & Rosenthal, F. (1967). *The Muqaddimah: An introduction to history*. Princeton, N.J: Princeton University Press.

Niazi, K. (1971). *Study of History*. Lahore, Pakistan: Hafeez Press.

Qasim, D. (2020, June 2019). *Session 1-8 – Reading Ibn Khaldun – Dr. Choukri*

Heddouchi. Youtube. https://www.youtube.com/watch?v=abqbFbwJyQc&list=PLTYBlyCxV Ip-FhyyYzIz4RgF28n2hMSzA

Rosenthal, F. (1968). *A History of Muslim Historiography*. Netherlands: E.J. Bell, Leiden.

Saleh, M.M.S. (2001). Developing a history curriculum: An Islamic perspective. *Intellectual Discourse*, 9(1), 85-100.

Siqqiqui, M. (1976). *Quranic Concept of History*. Islamabad: Islamic Research Institute, International Islamic University.

Taylor, T., & Young, C. (2003). *Making History: A Guide for Teaching and Learning of History in Australian Schools*. Victoria, Australia: Curriculum Corporation.

Toynbee, A.J. (1935). *A Study of History* (2nd ed.). London.

Vann, R. T. (2020, October 27). *Historiography*. Encyclopedia Britannica. Retrieved from https://www.britannica.com/topic/historiography

CHAPTER 5

Learning to Excel at Reading and Writing

Jameela Ho

This chapter is not about how to teach children reading and writing skills. Instead, it will be about the general processes of reading and writing. It will also include the educational theories behind learning to excel at each.

Reading and writing are two separate skills even though without writing there can be no reading. As such, there will be two separate sections focusing on each.

READING

"Read, in the Name of your Lord Who created—" and so begins the commandment of Allah ﷻ to our beloved Prophet Muhammad, peace and blessings be upon him (Quran, 96:1). What distinguishes humankind from other creations is his knowledge. Thus, Allah ﷻ had given Prophet Adam, peace be upon him, the first man, the knowledge of things:

He taught Adam the names of all things then He presented them to the angels and said Tell Me the names. (Quran, 2:31).

Knowledge can be gained from revelation, thinking, listening or reading. This is why reading is one of the important aspects of gaining knowledge.

Reading Theories

There are two basic reading theories that are at the opposite ends of each other. In the past one has been more dominant than the other in the teaching of reading. After a period of time the other became dominant. This is because people can't decide which one is better. However, it's not that one is better than the other but that both are equally important. The teaching of reading should incorporate both to cater to the needs of each child (Fletcher, Savage, & Vaughn, 2020). Understanding these two reading theories and using them in your teaching will help your children immensely.

Bottom-Up View

Other names for this theory is code-based, skills-based, the phonics approach or behavioural view. Children are taught how to decode words by learning the alphabet, phonics, blending, word recognition and other sub-skills. Reading is viewed as a linear process, building upon previous skills sequentially. When the reader has mastered all the skills then he or she is able to understand what was read. The end goal is to reach reading comprehension. One criticism of this view is that it does not take into account the context of reading and how the reader makes meaning through interacting with the text.

Since the turn of the 21st century, there have been many research that found phonics to be associated with reading success (Schatschneider, Fletcher, Francis, Carlson & Foorman, 2004; Shapiro & Solity, 2008). A decade later, research still finds that when children who had problems with decoding phonics are taught to master it then their reading success increases (Double, McGrane, Stiff, & Hopfenbeck, 2019).

Top-Down View

This view is also known as whole-language or the cognitive view. Reading is a process of making meaning using the reader's knowledge of language syntax (sentence structure), semantics (meaning) and cues. The emphasis is on the reader using the context of a piece of text to recognise words and meanings. Reading activities are designed based on the reader's experiences and knowledge. The main criticism of this view is that it ignores the teaching of the alphabet and how to decode it. Children are expected to understand how it works by interacting with words and books.

This way of teaching reading is very motivating for children because it caters to their needs and levels. Children are encouraged to use language naturally and playfully. They can invent their own spelling as they learn to spell properly (Gentry, 1987). Language is used as an integrated whole across subjects when studying themes or units of study instead of rote learning separate skills (Kolstad & Bardwell, 1997).

In Practice

In this section I will give an example of the difference of being in a skills-based classroom and in a whole language classroom. I draw upon the experiences of my elder sisters and that of my brother and myself. My sisters were older than me so they entered school in a skills-based era while my brother and I entered school during the shift towards a whole language classroom.

One of the differences in the skills-based approach and the whole language approach is the teaching of grammar. My sisters were in Years 4, 5 and 6 and recalled being drilled with grammar lessons. My brother and I, on the other hand, cannot remember a single grammar lesson. I had no idea what a subject or object was in a sentence nor did I know what were adverbial clauses and phrases. I could edit friends and family's works when asked but I could not explain to them why it needed correcting. To me, if it looked and sounded right then it was right. I was so used to using the words and sentences in context that it would look and sound odd if it wasn't correct. Meanwhile, my sisters could explain about auxiliary verbs but they had difficulties choosing the right ones in a sentence. When I started teaching, I had to quickly read through a grammar book to familiarise myself with all the grammar terms.

Fast forward the years to the time that I was teaching children to read. How did I teach my prekindergarten and kindergarten students to read? A mix of both approaches. The children were taught the alphabet and letter sounds in a fun way with singing rhymes and searching for familiar items starting with the letter sound. I catered to children's individual differences as those who were ready were taught the next skills but those who weren't were engaged in extended letter sound activities. There were daily shared reading of books that children looked forward to. They would listen raptly to the stories and often asked for another one to be read. Children in their spare time would reach for a book on the book shelf to 'read' to themselves or to their friends. Their 'reading' was actually a retelling of the story as they turned the pages of the book.

Having taught young children to read using phonics in a whole language class, I've witnessed their success at reading. Parents would in later years relate how well their children were doing in school, often winning awards for high achievements. Praise be to Allah ﷻ and may He ﷻ bless them.

Reading Skills

To be able to read, a person needs to recognise words and comprehend what those words mean. Within these two processes, there are multiple skills to master. For word recognition, children will need to learn the sound that a letter symbol makes, combine the letters and sounds to form and pronounce words and recognise word patterns. For reading comprehension, children will need to learn what each word means, have an extensive vocabulary, be fluent in the rate of reading and accurate, understand the context of the writing, have knowledge of various texts, and background knowledge of various topics.

For reading to happen, all these skills have to work smoothly and simultaneously. When it doesn't, children will struggle with reading. However, each skill is taught separately as children start schooling. As children progress, the next skill is taught.

It's beyond the scope of this chapter to go into these reading skills. Look out for my learning to read and write book where I discuss these skills in details.

Context and Semantics

All text has a purpose. It could be to entertain, convince, inform, question and so on (more on this in the writing section on text types). This is the context of the piece of writing or book. When a person reads, understanding the purpose of the writing makes it easier to understand the meaning of what is read. Rickett, Davies, Masterton, Stuart and Duff (2016) found that semantic knowledge and context helps with word reading among six year olds.

Early Reading Experiences

Reading to your children before they can read will help them to develop a love for reading. The time spent on your lap with a story makes it a special bonding time. Your children will look forward to it eagerly and will associate reading with happy memories.

Children who are read to regularly at a young age also tend to do well academically. Specifically, research found that children who are read to as early as 2 to 3 years of age had higher academic results in a standardised national test at 8 to 9 years of age (Shahaeian, Wang, Tucker-Drob, Geiger, &. Harrison, 2018). The more children are read to the better their results. Even reading routinely at bed time to children early in their young life predicted their academic skills in kindergarten and later on in Year 9 (Camara-Costa, Pulgar, Cusin, Labrell, & Dellatolas, 2021).

Schedule some time during the day and also at bedtime to read to your children!

What and How to Read to Children

Any good book is a good book to read to your children. But if you want to also teach children about Islam and Islamic morals and manners then read Islamic books. There are many Muslim authors to choose from these days and many variety of books for Muslim children.

You cannot always tell what is in a non-Muslim book. Some concepts are contrary to Islamic teachings even if subtly told. Having said that, some Muslim books do have non-Islamic concepts. The only way to know is to read the book yourself first or read Islamic book reviews by Muslim librarians, teachers and parents. There are websites and Instagram accounts set up for this. They will tell you what's inside the books so it'll save you time and you can make the judgement of whether you want your child to read them or not.

The early years before schooling is from birth to 5 years. There is a wide and diverse range of developmental needs during this period. The books you choose for a baby is different to a toddler and different to a pre-schooler. The way you read at each stage is also going to be different. There's a lot of information and it's beyond the scope of this chapter also.

For details on what to read to children and how to read to children at different ages from birth to 5 years of age, enrol into my online program, Nurturing the Love of Reading: The First 5 Years. Go here: https://jameela-ho-parenting-education.thinkific.com/courses/nurturing-the-love-of-reading-the-first-5-years

For older school age children, there are graded or levelled readers that can help with reading. These are books that are graded based on the degree of difficulty. When children start to read, the books they read will be graded easy. As they progress and improve, they advance to the more difficult books. You can match these books to your child's level of independent reading. Children usually understand more than what they can read. For reading to your child (even for younger children), choose any book that are about two levels above their reading ability. This will expose them to more difficult language, words and sentences.

Teaching Strategies

Shared Reading

Shared reading is also called modelled reading. Yes, it's a time for sharing books together but it's also where you can model how you read and help your children to think about the text and its meaning.

When you have your child comfortably on your lap or next to you, you begin first by looking at the front cover. You can comment about it based on the illustration and the title. So you might say, "Oh look at this boy – what's he doing? It looks like he's flying a kite. The title of the book says 'Ahmad's Kite.' This story must be about a little boy named Ahmad and his kite. I wonder if it's a new kite?" You can have your child answer any questions you ask.

You then read the book and stopping to look at the pictures. You might even look at some illustrations first to ask your child to predict what will happen next before you read the text on that page. When there is a difficult word you can discuss what it means then you might use a few of the synonyms in that sentence.

For older children, you might focus on sight words, grammar and punctuation in the text. For example, you might prepare beforehand by writing down some sight words in the book onto flashcards. Then after you finished reading you might ask your child to look for those sight words in the book. You can also play various games with those sight word flashcards.

After reading the book, you might have a discussion about the theme of the book. For example with Ahmad's Kite, you might say, "This book is not only about Ahmad's kite, is it? What happened when the little girl's kite broke? What did Ahmad do?" He shared his kite with her. It's about sharing so you might then discuss what it means to share. This is where Islamic books are great to read from. You can help your child to think deeper with discussions on characters, behaviours, morals and manners.

Guided Reading

For older school age children who are struggling with reading then you might do guided reading with them. This is where you help your children use any reading strategies that they've learnt. You sit with your child and listen to him or her read. When difficulties arises then you prompt, question or have a discussion about the word or text.

For example, if your child is having difficulties reading a word then you might help him or her to sound the word out by looking at the first letter or any letters that they know and try to blend or decode them. Or it could be to look at the spelling pattern or word family that the word belongs to. If it is a sight word then you might help your child to learn and memorise it. This is prompting your child to use reading skills to decode the word.

Another example is where your child has read the word wrong. You might ask, "Does that word makes sense there? Does that sound right in a sentence?" This is using the context to help him or her to make corrections.

Independent Reading

Have a bookcase with a selection of books. Make sure there are many Islamic titles there as well as classic and popular titles. From a young age, allow children to choose their own books to 'read' independently. The young ones will look at the illustrations. The pre-schoolers will try to retell the story. For older school age children, make sure you have a good selection of Islamic books, both fiction and non-fiction. Depending on what school your child goes to, most books read at school will be non-Muslim books. It'll be good for your child to have access to Islamic books.

Independent reading allows older children to follow their interests. If they read something that they're interested in then they will actually enjoy reading. I tutored a boy who loved anything about dinosaurs. He knew everything there was to know about them. He used to read whatever he could get his hands on about them. His parents, however, did not want him to read about dinosaurs. They'd had enough of listening to dinosaurs and wanted him to learn about other things. So they forbade him to read dinosaur books. He no longer had access to those books anymore. He hated reading other books because they weren't interesting. I told the parents that it's better that he's reading something than not read at all. In the meantime, they can try to expand his interests by introducing him to new and different things. Once a new interest takes place then he'll be wanting to read about that. The aim is to help your child find what he or she is interested in.

Reading Activities

Here are some activities that you might like to do with your children to encourage a love for reading.

1. Read to your children every day. Give your babies, cloth books. Point out things on that cloth book and say what it is. Give your toddlers board books. Point to things on that board book and say what it is. Give your pre-schoolers picture books. Put them on your lap and start reading.

2. Start a bedtime routine. After cleaning up and changing, settle them into bed. Select an Islamic book and read. Depending on age, start a little reflection/discussion based on the book. Recite bedtime surahs and duas. Kiss good night.

3. Tell stories to your children, especially Islamic stories from hadeeth or Quran. There are many stories that are not in book form that you can simplify and tell your children. Tell traditional stories. Children will pick up on language, vocabulary and meaning.

4. To raise phonemic awareness, play I Spy with your children. You can focus on the sound of the word by saying, "I spy with my little eyes something beginning with b-b-b (not letter b but the sound of b)." You can then help your children by asking, "It's a b-b-b-ball!" Once children are familiar with playing you can then ask "Do you think it's a s-s-s-sock?" – "No, I'm looking for b-b-b not s-s-s." "Do you think it's a b-b-b-bird?" "Yes! Bird starts with b-b-b."

5. Another phonemic awareness activity is to sing or read nursery rhymes. Better still, read Islam ones or make your own. Let your children fill in the next rhyme. Say "The cat sat on the –" and let your children say the next word. At first you might have to give your child some prompts. You can say "Where did the cat sat? Which word sounds like sat? Is it on the table, mat or rug?" The more rhymes your children hear then the more they'll know which ones rhymes.

6. Look for print in the environment. Point them out to your children – on the breakfast table, at the shops, on billboards, in the mail and so on. Play What Does it Say? Point to the milk carton and say "This says milk." Point to the jam and ask what does that say?

7. Go to the local library, read some books and borrow some books. You could also go to second hand book stores or even charity stores where they have books for sale. You can find great titles that are still in great condition for a couple of dollars or less.

8. Assign ten minutes independent reading time for everyone in the house. It could be after breakfast, after dinner when everyone is together or a time that's convenient for everyone. No one does anything, not even talking, except read for those ten minutes.

9. As a special reward, you can take your child to a bookstore and let him or her select any book they want. This is instead of buying toys or food as a reward.

10. Let your children be authors. Make up stories and make them into books. Your young children can dictate to you the stories and you can write them onto paper and staple them together. Let your children illustrate. For older children encourage them to write their own stories and

illustrate the books. Put them on the book shelf and you and your children can select and read them.

WRITING

Writing starts with holding a pencil or marker. The first step is to encourage your toddler to hold a writing instrument and make scribbles. Do this every day until he or she is ready for the next step. The next step is when they start to form the shapes of letters and practice writing the letters. This will happen when your child has better control of the writing implement and can hold it with a pincer grip. Once letters are mastered and they start to read and spell words phonetically and learn a few sight words then they can begin to write sentences. After this it's about learning vocabulary, spelling and grammar…and improving handwriting.

The Writing Process

Writing can be thought of as a process of steps to go through. There are about five steps.

1. Pre-writing. Before actually writing, it needs to be planned. This is where brainstorming and researching of the topic are done. What will the text be about? What will the layout look like? What will be the sub-headings that will guide the writing through to the end? Knowing the purpose and audience of the writing will determine the text type or genre to use and how to structure it.

2. Writing. It is time to write the first draft. It doesn't have to be perfect as it's only the first draft. The aim is to write all the ideas down into sentences then paragraphs and sections or chapters.

3. Edit. Once writing is completed, editing takes place. The first edit is to make changes to any content that doesn't make sense. The whole piece of text should be logical and flows smoothly from start to finish. The next edit is to proofread to correct any spelling or grammar errors.

4. Revise. Make all the necessary changes from the editing process. Read through it again and update any further changes.

5. Publish. Print the text or press publish to share the writing with others.

Research has found that planning and revising or editing leads students to higher quality writing (Limpo, Alves & Fidalgo, 2014). These are two important steps that most new writers tend not to engage in. Children often write from whatever comes off their head and when they're done, they don't reread what they've written. Planning will give focus and direction to a piece of writing. It will give the writer a chance to collect information and organise ideas. Revising and editing will improve the writing and make it stronger.

Types of Texts

There are many text types. These are the more common ones that children will encounter: narrative, recount, procedure, informational report, explanation, discussion and exposition. The purpose of knowing the different text types is to understand that each one serves a different purpose and audience. Also, each one has its own particular organisational structure and grammatical features.

For example, the narrative purpose is to entertain so the structure has a beginning where characters are introduced, the middle has a complication and the ending has a resolution. The exposition's purpose, on the other hand, is to persuade the reader of the writer's view so the structure has an introduction that states the viewpoint and introduce the arguments, the middle has the various arguments in logical order and then a conclusion to sum up the arguments. Knowing these differences will help make writing easier and more purposeful.

Bloom's Taxonomy and Writing

Bloom's taxonomy is a hierarchy of thinking and learning. It starts from the lowest level of thinking which is to remember and recall facts to create and produce something new or original.

It is a helpful tool for teachers to extend the learning or assess students. It can be used for any subject.

For writing, it is useful for guiding the writing to reach its highest form.

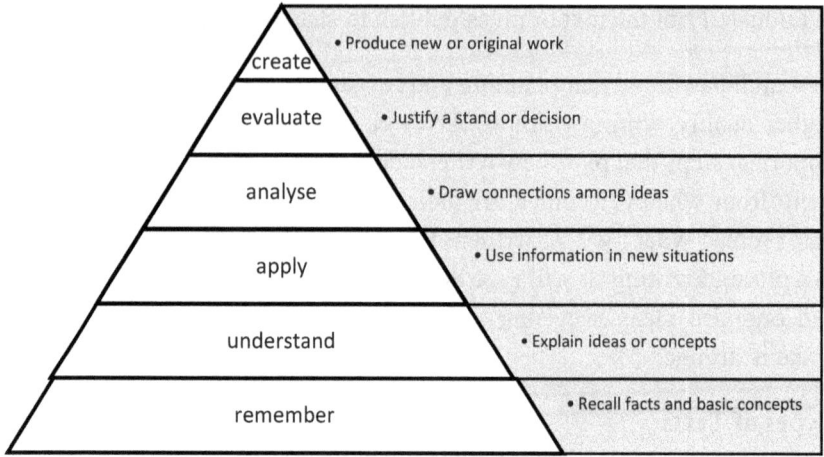

Diagram 1. Bloom's Taxonomy (see www.bloomstaxonomy.net **for details)**

Writing in the early grades will only require children to remember and understand. As children move into the later grades, they are expected to apply and even analyse what they write. The senior grades and university levels will require students to evaluate the topic they're writing about or create a unique piece such as a thesis. If your child is in university and getting low grades for his or her writing then you might look at Bloom's Taxonomy chart and ask if the writing has argued, critiqued and provided support of an issue instead of just explaining about the topic. Young children can also be taught to write beyond the recalling of facts and describing of ideas. Teach them how to apply this knowledge in their writing and even compare and contrast it.

Writing Activities

Here are some writing activities to help your child learn to love writing.

1. For young children not yet school age, let them make marks with different writing implements. This will give them plenty of practice holding with a pincer grip.

2. For school age children, practice handwriting every day. When letters are formed automatically, writing becomes easier. Do copy work from the Quran translation or hadith. This way your children will get both handwriting practice and also learn or memorise something new from

Islam. Select interesting and appropriate verses.

3. Read widely as reading will give ideas on what and how to write.

4. Keep a writing journal and write in it every day. Spend at least ten minutes. Write whatever comes to mind. It could be free flowing, brainstorming a topic or a poem or a thought. The aim is to get into the habit of writing every day.

5. Make "junk journals". Instead of buying journals, make them yourself. Find any type of paper and bundle them together. Find some cardboard for the cover (example, cereal boxes and decorate both sides) and staple or sew the bundle of papers and cover together. You can make them as simple or as fancy as you like. Let your child write in them!

6. Publish your children's writings. Encourage your children to write a book and have it published. It could be a compilation of short stories, poetry or opinion pieces. There is nothing like seeing your book in print to encourage you to write more and write better. There are many print-on-demand companies that will print books at cost for authors. For example, join KDP Amazon as an author and you can upload your children's books. Once it's uploaded then you can order the author's copy. This will be printed at cost and you just pay for postage as well. Total cost could be less than $10 a book (this will depend on if Amazon prints in your country).

7. Do your children have a favourite book? Why not write a review of it to recommend it to others? When children like something they'll want to talk, or in this case, they'll want to write about it.

8. For older children, ask them to write an essay (exposition or discussion) on Islamic topics such as, why is Islam the answer to life's problems? Why is kindness important in Islam? How does the spreading of salams lead to brotherhood? Make sure that, the writing is not just describing or explaining. Also make sure to go through the planning and editing process.

9. Challenge your children to write an Islamic children's book. It could be a narrative, a set of procedures (recipes or instructions on how to do something that they're really into), an informational report on an Islamic

topic such as the History of Andulusia, Muslim countries or anything that they're really into or a recount (a memoir of funny things that happened to them and that has some Islamic morals). The topic is really open to your children's interests. Once it's done, have it illustrated by your children (or a professional artist) then edit it professionally. Put it on Amazon and sell it (and get some author's copies as well).

References

Camara-Costa, H., Pulgar, S., Cusin, F., Labrell, F., & Dellatolas, G. (2021). Associations of language-based bedtime routines with early cognitive skills and academic achievement: A follow-up from kindergarten to middle school. *British Journal of Developmental Psychology, 39*, 521–539.

Double, K.S., McGrane, J.A., Stiff, J.C., & Hopfenbeck, T.N. (2019). The importance of early phonics improvements for predicting later reading comprehension. *British Educational Research Journal, 45* (6), 1220–1234.

Fletcher, J.M., Savage, R., & Vaughn, S. (2020). A commentary on Bowers and the role of phonics instruction in reading. *Educational Psychology Review, 33,* 1249–1274.

Gentry, J.R. (1987). From traditional to whole language teaching. *Teaching Pre K-8, 17*(8), 38

Kolstad, R., & Bardwell, J. (1997). Phonics vs. whole language reading in the teaching of reading. *Reading Improvement, 34*(4), 154.

Limpo, T., Alves, R.A., & Fidalgo, R. (2014). Children's high-level writing skills: Development of planning and revising and their contribution to writing quality. *British Journal of Educational Psychology, 84*, 177–193.

Rickett, J., Davies, R., Masterton, J., Stuart, M., & Duff, F.J. (2016). Evidence for semantic involvement in regular and exception word reading in emergent readers of English. *Journal of Experimental Child Psychology*, 150, 330–345.

Schatschneider, C., Fletcher, J.M., Francis, D.J., Carlson, C.D., & Foorman, B.R. (2004). Kindergarten prediction of reading skills: A longitudinal comparative analysis. *Journal of Educational Psychology, 96* (2), 265–282.

Shahaeian, A., Wang, C., Tucker-Drob,V., Geiger, E., Bus, A.G., &. Harrison, L.J. (2018). Early shared reading, socioeconomic status, and children's cognitive and school competencies: six years of longitudinal evidence. *Scientific Studies of Reading, 22*(6), 485–502.

Shapiro, L.R. & Solity, J. (2008). Delivering phonological and phonics training within whole-class teaching. *British Journal of Educational Psychology, 78,* 597–620.

CHAPTER 6
Utilising Learning Differences
Taherah Moslih

In the current day, there are many methods of teaching and beliefs about learning. However, they all have one thing in common; they stress the importance of a single strategy, thus massing together every child as one. Making education accessible to only certain groups means making it inaccessible to the rest. In Islam, education is of utmost importance and is a foundation of our deen. The Quran so often calls on us to learn, use our wisdom and to think. Indisputably, then, we cannot uphold this Islamic value without ensuring that every person- particularly every child- is given an equal opportunity to learn by being catered to by different teaching strategies. The purpose of my teaching is to be inclusive of every unique learner, regardless of learning styles, learning difficulties or background. In the following pages I will approach the subject of learning differences and how we may cater to them in teaching both the school curriculum and Islam.

How Does The Typical Brain Learn And Remember?

Learning is a process of forming permanent pathways in the brain so that new knowledge or skills are remembered. Children are born with about 100 billion neurons in the brain (Novak, 2019). As a child learns something new, the neurons that are involved in the process connect with one another. This connection grows stronger and more efficient every time that neural pathway is used. Meanwhile, old connections that are no longer needed may be cut in order to make room for more efficient learning. This ability of the brain to change and adapt is referred to as 'neuroplasticity'; a significant element of childhood development.

Although learning uses neurons all across the brain, different types of learning will occur primarily in respective areas of the brain, called "lobes." For example, parts of the temporal lobe are in charge of understanding language, while the frontal lobe is where we store numerical knowledge for math. This forms a network of highly integrated yet organised learning systems.

In order to learn, the brain must undergo 3 processes of memorisation; encoding, storage and retrieval. Encoding occurs as the brain absorbs and processes sensory information. Once we pay conscious attention to that input, we can transfer it into memory storage. Once stored in long-term memory, retrieval allows us to bring that information back into our conscious attention, ready to be used.

These are the fundamental principles of the typical brain as it learns.

What Is A Learning Difficulty?

It is important first to distinguish between a learning disability and a learning difficulty. A learning disability is a severe condition which affects IQ and all other areas of life. A learning difficulty is a difference in the way a person learns which becomes a hurdle in a typical learning environment, but does not affect IQ. Learning disabilities require special care and support, and will not be the focus of this chapter. Rather, we will break down the learning differences that are disadvantaged because they not appropriately catered to. In particular, we will focus on learning difficulties called 'neurodivergencies' that are diagnosable and relatively common.

Neuroplasticity is evidence that learning difficulties can be worked with to still allow effective learning (Turton, 2013). Every learner is unique, with their own strengths and needs. However, by understanding different neurodivergencies, we may effectively teach those who struggle with them rather than leaving them behind. This needs to begin at the very early ages, as this is when the brain is most plastic and learning difficulties are most easily catered to.

We will learn about 3 of the most common neurodivergencies—ADHD, ASD and Dyslexia—and how to cater to them in our teaching.

What Is ADHD?

ADHD (Attention Deficit Hyperactive Disorder) affects at least 1/20 people globally and at least a further 1/20 experience the same symptoms but not to an extent that is diagnosable (Sayal, et al., 2018). All factors considered, the real proportion of the population with ADHD is assumed to be higher, as ADHD tends to go under-diagnosed, particularly in girls. In order to be diagnosed with ADHD, a psychologist must use a set of criteria outlined in the DSM-5 (5th ed.; DSM–5; American Psychiatric Association, 2013) to decide whether ADHD is an accurate verdict. The criterion includes a range of examples of inattention, hyperactivity and impulsivity, all of which have to have been present across several environments for over 6 months and to an extent that disrupts one's daily life. By breaking down just these most common symptoms found in the DSM-5, we see the impacts that ADHD has on a student's learning. Inattention causes a difficulty listening to teachers and classmates, being forgetful of homework or being unable to complete tasks that have been set. Hyperactivity makes it difficult to sit still at a desk to complete work. Impulsivity leads to disruptive behaviour. In just these three basic symptoms of ADHD, the impact on learning is evident.

How Can We Cater For ADHD In Teaching Curriculum?

Environment

Reducing the colourful posters, decor and toys all around the classroom reduces the chances of diverted attention from those with ADHD. The overdone visual stimuli is also a cause of over-stimulation for any student, and even more so for ADHD learners. Over-stimulation is a root cause of most cases of hyperactivity and agitation you might find in a classroom.
Restricting students to a cross-legged position on the floor or on plastic chairs gives no room for movement for students who require frequent movement. Rather than them fidgeting while you talk, incorporate movement within lessons by playing educational games away from the desk. (Go to my Instagram for some fun ideas: https://www.instagram.com/easyteaching.melb/guide/off-the-desk-learning/17895501746505173)

Techniques

Students with ADHD tend to have a stronger primary learning style than most. It is also more common for their primary learning style to be kinaesthetic. Try to teach often through tactile resources such as blocks, toys, board games or objects in nature.
The inattentive symptom also makes it difficult to focus when someone is speaking. Reduce time spent verbally explaining tasks and instead teach by example, diagrams or written instructions.

Tools

Most educators are bringing fidget toys into the classroom to cater for ADHD learners. While this helps with feelings of anxiety and agitation, it does not necessarily aide learning. As well as incorporating movement in lessons, try to bring in alternative seating such as exercise balls that allow movement without diverting attention.

How can we cater for ADHD in teaching Islam?

Salah

It is common for children with ADHD to rush prayer, be distracted by sounds and let their eyes wander. It is essential to teach them the skills to avoid distraction young. First, implement 'centering time' before every prayer. This will be a time where they take deep breaths, make intention to pray the salah, focus on their relationship with Allah ﷻ and really zone into the moment before beginning their prayer.
Another greatly beneficial tool is to understand the words and motions of salah. Utilise the highly active and plastic brain during childhood to teach the meanings of dua's and surahs that are used in prayer. This way, salah becomes a meaningful interaction that they are attentive to, rather than a series of actions and words that are easy to zone out of.

Quran

As with teaching curriculum, teaching Quran to children with ADHD should be approached with their learning differences in mind. Memory impairments make it difficult to memorise Quran the way a typical learner might. Instead, try using visual games. Here are some you can try out:

Connecting Quran:
Write out a surah, broken up into its ayahs (or smaller parts) onto seperate pieces of paper. Have them put the pieces together in the correct order to complete the surah.

Dictation:
Read out the surah to them little-by-little. Have them try to write it out in English (transliteration) in the way that they hear it. This can then be what they use to practise the surah.

What is ASD?

As ASD (Autism spectrum disorder) is a spectrum, it will vary in degree for every person and symptoms shown across each person. There are, however, some common symptoms that are experienced by most of those who are diagnosed. The first of these is a sensory overload (Wiggins, et al., 2009). Sensory overload occurs when the brain is receiving too much information from the five senses and is unable to sort through and process it effectively, causing agitation and difficulty focusing.

Another characteristic symptom of autism is a social impairment (Leung, et al., 2016), where one's ability to pick up on social cues in order to respond appropriately is impaired and it is difficult to learn the appropriate gestures, facial expressions and language to communicate. This deprives students with ASD of social learning; one of the most effective ways to learn (Ladd, 1981). It also becomes challenging to make friends, leading to bullying from peers, an issue exacerbated by another recurrent symptom of ASD- 'stimming' (Rajagopalan, et al., 2013). Stimming refers to small repetitive movements that the body uses to self-regulate when feeling unsettled. It may show up as leg-bouncing, shaking out their hands, or tugging at their hair. As these movements are atypical, they are often met with discomfort, judgement, fear and more bullying.

Finally, there is a hyper-rigidity component of ASD that makes it difficult to be flexible in routines and behaviours (DSM-5). Changes to regular routine or to expectations can be extremely untethering and may lead to meltdowns by autistic students.

All of these symptoms make learning in a typical environment considerably challenging.

How can we cater for ASD in teaching curriculum?

To address this, we will consider each of the aforementioned symptoms of ASD students and how they may be catered to.

Sensory overload

Again, it is beneficial to reduce clutter and too much decor in a learning environment. While posters and learning resources stimulate a child's mind, an excess will only over-stimulate the brain, an experience that ASD learners are more prone to due to their heightened senses.

Hard plastic chairs or the hard floor may cause a discomfort that is highly amplified for ASD learners, thus detrimental to their learning. Opt for seating options such as exercise balls, swivel chairs, cushions on the floor, etc., ensuring that their feet are always settled and not hanging. A comfortable sensory experience is the key to making learning easier for children with ASD.

Social Impairments

While social learning is one of the most effective modes of learning, there are considerations to be made with learners on the spectrum. In a classroom, seating arrangements should be designed in a manner that encourages social learning but still allows for independent learning without the pressure of socialising. This could be circular tables that are large enough to allow each student plenty of personal space, or tables arranged in a U-shape around the classroom in a way that is collaborative but does not force interaction.

When conducting group projects, make the role of each student very clear to avoid the social stress that a student with ASD may experience. Once they are clear on their task, it is easier to communicate their progress with the rest of the group.

Hyper-rigidity

It is not practical to ensure completely rigid routines in learning for the comfort of autistic students. Instead, find flexibility within routines and encourage simple habits.

"Do good deeds properly, sincerely and moderately and know that your deeds will not make you enter Paradise, and that the most beloved deed to Allah is the most regular and constant even if it were little" [Sahih Bukhari]

For example, establish a routine of subjects to be taught each day, but allow changes within the subject as needed. The consistency in subject routine allows learners with ASD to feel comfortable and prepared whilst the way in which each subject is taught may vary and change.
To set them on the right path for the rest of the day, establish a morning routine before classes begin. This could look something like:

Student walks in every morning and picks up his favourite book. He sits in the beanbag in the same corner and reads for 20 minutes. He then comes to his table and takes out his books/pencils for the day.

By starting the day with comfortable routines, a learner with ASD is in a better mental and emotional state to begin learning.

How can we cater for ASD in teaching Islam?

<u>Salah</u>

Thankfully, praying on time can become an easy habit for learners with ASD due to their advanced sense of time and adherence to routine. However, the experience of prayer can become very uncomfortable for those with heightened senses. Clothes can feel too itchy, standing and covering the body can make the body temperature rise, sounds and scents can become extremely distracting. It is important to make changes that reduce these factors as much as possible so that prayer is not associated with discomfort from an early age.
To begin with, establish an area for prayer (a room, corner, etc). This space will be reserved for prayer alone. It should have no visual distractions. Attempt to make it as comfortable as possible (I like to use a foam prayer mat).

After the external environment is established, teach them practises to observe before prayer such as wearing clothes they are comfortable in and avoiding any perfume or strong soaps that may distract them. In teaching them to establish these habits on their own, you are setting them up to make salah easier on them in any environment as they get older.

Quran

Overstimulation can make it difficult to read Quran with its many symbols and often tightly-packed calligraphy. When teaching ASD readers to learn Quran, use Qurans with colour-coded rules, or highlight all tajweed symbols in a different colour to visually separate them from the letters. This clear distinction makes it easier for the autistic brain to absorb what they are looking at, as well as avoiding the loss of focus that comes from overstimulation.

Social

Being friendly and connecting with our community is an essential practise of a Muslim.

At-Tabarani narrated in al-Mu'jam al-Awsat (4422) that Abu Sa'eed al-Khudri said: The Messenger ﷺ of Allah ﷻ said: "The most perfect of the believers in faith are those who are best in manners and attitude, who are humble, who feel at ease with people and people feel at ease with them. He is not one of us who does not feel at ease with people and they do not feel at ease with him."

Al-Bukhari (12) and Muslim (29) narrated from 'Abdullah ibn 'Amr (may Allah have mercy on him) that a man asked the Prophet (blessings and peace of Allah be upon him): What part of Islam is best? He said: "To feed others, and to greet with salaam those whom you know and those whom you do not know."

However, we know that ASD may cause social impairments, affecting both the giving and the receiving of social niceties. Here is how we can work with this learning difference:

- Actively teach social cues that are learnt naturally by the typical learner. You may do this by presenting photos of facial expressions and learning what emotion they are expressing.
- Practise social habits so that they become natural rather than uncomfortable social interactions. This may include practising saying salam to every Muslim they meet, smiling at anyone they make eye contact with, or rehearsed greetings.
- Teach them how to set their own boundaries. Allow them to tell others confidently if they do not want to be hugged or need to be left alone for a moment. In empowering them in their own choices, you are making them feel safe enough to approach social situations without fear.

What is Dyslexia?

Like ASD, Dyslexia occurs on a spectrum and can therefore differ in the way it is expressed and its severity (Shaywitz, 2020). For a long time, it has been considered a specific learning disorder that seemed to directly impact IQ. Due to this lack of understanding of the realities of dyslexia, students struggling with it have been often left behind - deemed a lost cause - which has led to behavioural issues in classrooms (Shaywitz, 2020). Research has now shown that it can occur across any range of intellectual abilities, has no direct effect on IQ and, although a barrier to learning, does not disable one's ability to learn (Reid, 2019).

The ability to read and write requires several neurological systems, all of which occur across multiple areas of the brain. Neuro-imaging studies have shown that those with dyslexia have less grey matter (the outer part of the brain consisting mostly of nerves) in the left parietotemporal area of the brain; this is the area of the brain responsible for consciously breaking down units of sounds (phonemes) in order to process reading. This is the method by with the neuro-typical brain learns to read and write.

How can we cater for dyslexia in teaching curriculum?

It has been determined that early diagnosis and intervention, alongside an understanding of dyslexic strengths, can compensate for dyslexic barriers and allow one to read and write effectively through atypical methods (Reid, 2019).

Tools

Technology use has been found to have great value as a method of assignment for students with dyslexia (Draffan, et al., 2007). It gives them an equal opportunity to participate in classwork and showcase their creativity without the restrictions of reading and writing. Rather than restricting students to posters/essays to present their research, allow them to use movie-journalling whereby they record videos using imagery and/or speech to present their message. Encourage the use of audio books, videos and apps to supplement some of the research and reading time so that their difficulty does not cause them to fall behind.

Technique

Dyslexia does not disable the ability to read and write. As the areas of the brain required to consciously break down phonemes are affected by dyslexia, dyslexic students may learn to read through systematically breaking them down. These are known as decoding skills. Decoding skills include the ability to recognise graphemes (letters or groups of letters) and phonemes (the sound made by each grapheme) as well as being able to break down words into these fragments of graphemes/phonemes. Decoding skills should be drilled so that they become automatic and effortless for the dyslexic learner, allowing them to read and write at a regular speed.

Here are some drilling practises you can try:

- Counting out the sounds they can hear in a spoken word

- Circling each grapheme in a written word

- Write a word on a card and have them cut it into its graphemes.

- Word endings: Put down a flashcard with a letter ("T"), then allow them to add cards with different endings ("IN", 'OP", "ALL") to make words ("TIN", "TOP", "TALL").

- Choosing the correct grapheme: Have them choose a flashcard with the correct spelling choice for a sound in a word (e.g. Write

R__D. Let them choose the flashcard "EE", "EA" or "I" to make the word "read"). This drills the concept of different spelling choices for each sound.

- Draw boxes for each sound in a word. Allow them to fill in the boxes with the correct spelling choice for each sound in the word. (Here is a free EasyTeaching worksheet to try this one out! Go to https://cdn.me-qr.com/pdf/4114776.pdf)

How can we cater for dyslexia in teaching Islam?

Quran:

A study by Ramli, et al. (2016) found that 79% of Muslim students surveyed that were suspected to suffer from dyslexia also struggled to read Quran. Therefore, it is essential that we do not neglect reading of the Quran with dyslexic students.

The Quran differs to English reading in three primary ways; letters are always pronounced the same way, letters look different in different parts of the word and there are symbols of tajweed alongside the letters. This means that regular drills in decoding will not be of use when reading Quran. Instead, these changes can be made for dyslexic students learning to read Quran:

- Find Quranic text in larger and more legible fonts.
- Have them write out every Arabic letter in its "beginning", "middle" and "ending" form into a table to promote fluency in letter recognition.
- Point out a letter one-by-one and have them make the corresponding sound.
- Begin reading without tajweed and focusing solely on sounding out each letter.
- Have them highlight symbols of tajweed and colour-code them for reading.
- Use multi-sensory reading strategies from a young age. This may include forming the letters of a word with play-dough, tracing words into sand or colouring in each letter of a word in a different colour.

In familiarising ourselves with the foundational knowledge of learning difficulties and making these small changes to our teaching practises, we are taking the first steps towards more inclusive education. However, we must continue to seek knowledge, acknowledge every student's individual differences and adapt continually in order to allow every child the opportunity to fulfil their Islamic duty of seeking knowledge.

Bibliography

American Psychiatric Association. (2013). *Diagnostic and statistical manual of mental disorders* (5th ed.). https://doi.org/10.1176/appi.books.9780890425596

Kleim, J. A., & Jones, T. A. (2008). Principles of Experience-Dependent Neural Plasticity: Implications for Rehabilitation After Brain Damage. *Journal of Speech, Language & Hearing Research*, *51*(1), S225–S239.

Ladd, G. W. (1981). Effectiveness of a social learning method for enhancing children's social interaction and peer acceptance. *Child Development, 52*(1), 171–178. https://doi.org/10.2307/1129227

Leung, R. C., Vogan, V. M., Powell, T. L., Anagnostou, E., & Taylor, M. J. (2016). The role of executive functions in social impairment in Autism Spectrum Disorder. *Child neuropsychology : a journal on normal and abnormal development in childhood and adolescence*, *22*(3), 336–344. https://doi.org/10.1080/09297049.2015.1005066

Rajagopalan, S. S., Dhall, A., & Goecke, R. (2013). Self-Stimulatory Behaviours in the Wild for Autism Diagnosis. *2013 IEEE International Conference on Computer Vision Workshops, Computer Vision Workshops (ICCVW), 2013 IEEE International Conference on, Computer Vision Workshops, International Conference On*, 755–761.

Sahih al-Bukhari 6463, Book 81, Hadith 52

Sayal, K., Prasad, V., Daley, D., Ford, T., & Coghill, D. (2018). ADHD in children and young people: prevalence, care pathways, and service provision. *Lancet.Psychiatry*, *5*(2), 175–186.

Shaywitz, S. (2012). *Overcoming dyslexia*. A.A. Knopf.

Turton, A.M. **and** Green, S. (2013), "Prevention Strategies for Students At-Risk for Learning Disabilities", Bakken, J.P., Obiakor, F.E. and Rotatori, A.F. (Ed.) *Learning Disabilities: Identification, Assessment, and Instruction of Students with LD (Advances in Special Education, Vol. 24)*, Emerald Group Publishing Limited, Bingley, pp. 109-128.

Wiggins, L. D., Robins, D. L., Bakeman, R., & Adamson, L. B. (2009). Brief report: sensory abnormalities as distinguishing symptoms of autism spectrum disorders in young children. *Journal of autism and developmental disorders, 39*(7), 1087–1091. https://doi.org/10.1007/s10803-009-0711-x

ABOUT THE AUTHORS

Chapter 1&5: Jameela Ho holds a Master of Education at Macquarie University, Sydney and a Master of Research from Western Sydney University. She is currently studying and researching factors that affect children's academic achievement. She blogs on the subject of both education and parenting, each on two separate blogs. ILMA Education (www.ilmaeducation.com) is where she motivates kids to excel at studying and learning. Her Muslim Parenting blog (www.jameelaho.com) is where she helps parents to raise kids with good morals, manners and behaviour.

Chapter 2: Aishah Ho is a mathematics teacher who holds a Master of Education at Macquarie University, Sydney. She was also the head of the Mathematics department at AlZahra College, an International Baccalaureate school. She has twenty years of teaching experience. Apart from being a high school mathematics teacher, she had also worked as a primary teacher teaching fourth grade to sixth grade. She had worked in public high schools as well as Muslim schools, teaching the state mathematics curriculum as well as the International Baccalaureate mathematics curriculum. Currently, she is working on the wonders of Allah's creations and its links to mathematics.

Chapter 3: Meenara Khan is a former math and science teacher from Chicago with 6 years of teaching experience in the United States and Pakistan. Raised in the USA, Meenara's experiences inspired her to create educational content that highlights Muslim/Islamic life and culture for classroom teaching. As a teacher, she believes hands-on, interactive learning for all ages is the key to engagement and happy classrooms. In 2020, she received her Masters in Biology for Science Educators from Clemson University, SC. Recently, she became a Cambridge Certified teacher with honors distinction. Meenara continues to provide professional teacher training in Pakistan and makes amazing Muslim/Islamic themed resources! Currently, she runs her online teacher business at The Hijabi Teacher.

Chapter 4: Mariam Seddiq is a history enthusiast who studied at the University of Sydney, Australia, specialising in Islamic civilisation and history. She also completed a postgraduate diploma in psychology from Monash University, Melbourne. She appreciates how interwoven the subjects of history and psychology are in deepening our understanding of people and society. For the past thirteen years, she has been busy teaching history to secondary school students and continues to pursue her research and writing through her website (www.medrese.be).

Chapter 5: Taherah Moslih studied at the University of Melbourne, majoring in neuroscience. Alongside learning about how the brain grows and develops she completed a certificate of Early Childhood Education and Care. She has been tutoring for 6 years, worked in childcare and is currently a Quran and Islamic Studies teacher at the PGCC Maktab. EasyTeaching (@easyteaching.melb) is where she teaches educators and parents about children's unique brains, learning differences and psychologically proven learning strategies.

www.ingramcontent.com/pod-product-compliance
Lightning Source LLC
Chambersburg PA
CBHW071315110426
42743CB00042B/2541